The Unbroken Web

Richard Adams
The Unbroken Web

Stories and Fables

Color plates by Yvonne Gilbert

Black and white drawings by Jennifer Campbell

CROWN PUBLISHERS, INC.   NEW YORK

By the same author

Watership Down
Shardik
The Plague Dogs
The Girl in a Swing

First published 1980 in the
United States of America by
Crown Publishers, Inc.

First published 1980 in Great Britain by
Allen Lane as *The Iron Wolf and Other Stories*

This book was designed and produced by Rizzoli Editore,
from an idea by Gabriele Pantucci.
Designer: Bernard Higton

Set in Monophoto Garamond
Printed and bound by Rizzoli Editore, Milan, Italy

ISBN: 0-517-542315

To my secretary, Janice Kneale,
with appreciation and gratitude

CONTENTS

THE UNBROKEN WEB

One morning a girl, not long married, was sweeping and dusting the bedroom. The vacuum cleaner, pushed under the bed, bumped into a suitcase, and Cynthia, going down on her knees beside the bed, pulled it out. It occurred to her that while she was about it, the suitcase might as well have a turn-out too, and she opened it and began sorting through the contents. Two minutes later she was kneeling among the rubbish, weeping bitterly and reading a small bundle of letters which revealed that her husband had been unfaithful to her.

When she tackled him James, all self-control, presented a flat surface, quietly and firmly insisting that he could not discuss the matter. Though recent, it was, he said, concluded, so she must put it out of her mind and never mention it again. Since, in his view, she now had nothing to worry about, this was obviously the sensible course. Cynthia, gentle and compliant by nature, tried to do as he asked, to suppress her feelings and to forget the whole thing.

Two months later, conversing with some friends (of whom I was one) about the unconscious mind, she related without any embarrassment the following dream, to support her contention that dreams were meaningless and nonsensical.

'I dreamt,' she said, 'that I had become a postman. I was standing at the foot of a wooded mountain, carrying a bag of letters which I had to deliver to a house at the top. As I climbed, the bag grew heavier and heavier, until at last I was forced to my knees and was dragging it along as best I could. I was determined to get the letters to their destination. It seemed a very dirty mountain. I was covered with dust and worse than dust. At last I came out on the top, and it was very lonely and bleak. I saw the house perched on the summit of the mountain, but as I approached I saw that it was like a stage prop. – two-dimensional and made only of plywood. As I stood wondering what to do, it collapsed and fell down the back of the mountain, and I awoke.'

With those who believe that dreams have no meaning, the transmutation of denied emotion into symbolic dream episodes is often so straightforward and clear as to need no analysis. A child could interpret poor Cynthia's dream, though she herself could not, because she was trying to suppress the emotion which had created it. Her unconscious mind knew better. Her feelings had to find an outlet. What is cause for wonder is the ingenuity of her unconscious in making use of the physical details of the actual experience – the kneeling, the letters, the dust and dirt – to create symbolic meaning.

I could tell several similar true stories of dreams. Cynthia's is not exceptional.

The weaving of emotion and experience into tales, therefore – or at least into corresponding incidents and visual images linked by a semblance of consequentiality – is a spontaneous and involuntary phenomenon. We do it naturally, we cannot help doing it and often the ingenuity with which we find we have done it is startling.

The connection between dreams and stories is inescapable. Like dreaming, making up stories based on emotion and experience is a universal phenomenon. As with dreams, the correspondence between experience and the created story often goes unrecognized. But there is an important difference. The dream is aimed only at a one-person audience – the dreamer – and therefore need not necessarily make sense in terms of that which we all have in common, realism and waking life: need not, in fact, conform with common sense. Hence the widespread belief that dreams are nonsense.

Tales, then, are similar to dreams, except that, since they are made to be shared, they have to take into account the circumstances of waking life – to be expressed, as it were, in the universal lingua franca. Nevertheless, they often sit loose to strict realism. In particular, folk-tales, by way of exciting interest and wonder in their audiences, commonly disregard questions of probability. Their hearers are happy to accept, within the framework of a story, things which they know to lie beyond realistic possibility. The prince has a magic horse: the princess's cat can talk, and so on. We are dreaming awake, and therefore such things have a meaning and value which we accept and may very well prefer to a strictly realistic tale. This is not true of folk-tales alone. No one believes in James Bond, his guns and girls and villains; in Piggy and Ralph on their island, in Yossarian and Milo Minderbender. Nevertheless, like dreams, they express something for us. They have meanings which we need, accept and welcome, and the very fact that they are only partially realistic is the essence of their attraction. Dreams are the individual's folk-tales and folk-tales are collective dreams. As Proust said, 'One cannot properly describe human life unless one shows it soaked in the sleep in which it plunges, which night after night sweeps round it as a promontory is encircled by the sea.'

I see in fancy – I have a vision of – the world as the astronauts saw it – a shining globe, poised in space and rotating on its polar axis. Round it, enveloping it entirely, as one Chinese carved ivory ball encloses another within it, is a second, incorporeal, gossamer-like sphere – the unbroken web – rotating freely and independently of the rotation of the earth. It is something like a soap-bubble, for although it is in rotation, real things are reflected on its surface, which imparts to them glowing, lambent colours.

Within this outer web we live. It soaks up, transmutes and is charged with human experience, exuded from the world within like steam or an aroma from cooking food. The story-teller is he who reaches up, grasps that part of the web which happens to be above his head at the moment and draws it down – it is, of course, elastic and unbreakable – to touch the earth. When he has told his story – its story – he releases it and it springs back and continues in rotation. The web moves continually above us, so that in time every point on its interior surface passes directly above every point on the surface of the world. This is why the same stories are found all over the world, among different people who can have had little or no communication with each other.

Both in folk-song and folk-tale there is a paradox. On the one hand they are not attributable to individual authors, but impersonal and universal. On the other, they lose much when they are depersonalized – the songs written down and played on the piano, the tales written down and made anonymous for reading in a book. A folk-song is best when sung by a flesh-and-blood singer to real listeners. A folk-tale is best when told aloud, spontaneously, at a particular time and place. This is like drinking wine or making love. That time is that time – unique and irrecoverable. The thing may be repeated, but that will be different – another occasion. Filming, printing and recording are inappropriate.

For this reason I have tried to give to each of these stories the semblance of a real setting. Each is supposedly told by a particular narrator to a hearer or hearers at a certain time and place and each is presented as growing out of the imagined time and place as a plant out of soil. Sometimes irony is present – that is, an unspoken correspondence between the story and the circumstances of the narrator and his hearers – but not in every case.

Folk-tales are, of course, less sophisticated than novels. As a rule there is not much dialogue. Protagonists are types rather than individuals. The prince is a prince and the dragon is a dragon like other dragons. As it seems to me, the tales' great qualities are two. First, they are full of surprises and marvels. The essence of fiction is that the hearer is dying to learn what happened next, or if he already knows, he is eager to hear it again and to take fresh delight in his wonder. Secondly, they are most admirably witty, neat and adroit. I only hope I have managed to retain these qualities. To take the stories to pieces as though on a bench, to examine them in detail and fit them together again, has been an enjoyable and happy experience. I have felt rather like a horologist or jeweller working on beautiful, antique musical-boxes, clocks or mechanical toys. How dexterous and well-made is this toy, this artifact, and how deftly it works! That part, which appears at first to have no particular function, is actually of vital importance. If you doubt it, just try taking it away! Times change, so perhaps that other part needs a touch of adjustment, but if so it must be done most carefully and respectfully.

And meaning? One can become too much preoccupied with meaning. What is the meaning of a rose? These stories are very old. In times past they have no doubt meant many different things to different people. Some meanings may well have disappeared for ever, together with the vanished circumstances of lives gone by. Today some of us, in our turn, perceive meanings in terms of the unconscious and its symbolism. In centuries to come the tales will still be there, but what they will then seem to mean we cannot tell. For the unbroken web has one other property, which I forgot to mention. It is impenetrable.

══The Cat in the Sea══

Let it alone, Master Richard! Come away from it this very minute, or I'll tell your mother, sure as I'm stood here! You just be a good boy, now! That's a jellyfish, that is, and you goes touching that, it'll sting you; and that'd be a right old end to your holiday, that would, and the mistress after me for letting it happen.

Anyways, you've done enough running about in the sun to last for a bit, specially if you wants a donkey-ride. The man'll be bringing them down on the sand in half hour or thereabouts. You come and sit down here in the shade – yes, and Miss Jean too, the both of you. I never did see such a pair of little Turks in all my life. I declare, if there was decorations for gettin' in a mess, I'd send you up to that there Lord George in London for a couple of putty medals, that I would! And he's got enough to give away, be all accounts, God bless him!

Now you just act right and stop kicking that sand about, and I'll tell you about the cat in the sea. For that was all along of the jellyfish, that was; and that's why the jellyfish goes floating about in the sea by himself and stings anyone that touches him. He's a proper bad lot, he is – always was, or my name's not Constance Cripps. Will you hold still now, Master Richard, while I comb this sand out of your hair? Dear oh law, one of these days we'll have to put you in with the funny man in the pierrot show; then you can earn

'undred pounds for a tuppenny grin. Hold still, now, Miss Jean, else I won't tell you about the jellyfish and the pussy-cat. Well, you pulls and it hurts – 'course it do. And salt water makes hair that sticky, it's like rakin' honey out of a doormat. There, that's better.

Well, now, long ago, you see, all the birds and animals could breathe under water as well as what they could on dry land, and the same t'other way round. That's to say, all the fishes and sea-creatures could come out of the water if they wanted to, and pay a visit to the land; and a funny sight it must have been, I should think, with fishes sitting up on stones by the sea, and horses and dogs all running down into the water and walking about down there like it was Greenham Common on a Sunday. But anyway, be all accounts it worked well enough and there was no complaints about elephants treading on mackerels' toes nor nothing o' that: and it might all have gone on very well from that day to this if it hadn't a' been for the jellyfish – very likely great-great-grandfather of that self-same jellyfish as I said you was to leave alone and very soon you'll hear why, Master Richard, if you'll just stop tryin' to pick a hole in that rug and listen to what I'm saying.

Well, the jellyfish was a nasty, spiteful creature then, just the same as he is now, and he kept on thinking wouldn't it be just about fine if he was

the only one as could go from the sea to the land and back again and none of the others able to do it at all: for then he'd have all the beaches of the world to himself, you see, and he'd be grander than wrasse, bass and dogfish put together. And at last he got so taken up with this idea that off he went for a year and a day to a great magician that lived at the other end of the world, and offered to steal him the sea king's emerald if only he'd give him a charm that would stop every living creature in the sea from being able to breathe on dry land. And he got it, too, but just what was the rights of that crooked old bargain no one else ever did know. It was all kept close like, and nothing to whisper nothing to dream, as the saying goes. But anyways, that emerald was found gone and a very funny thing that was too, for the sea king used to keep it in a cupboard of coral that had just one crack in it and that was so narrow that nothing could ever have squeezed through it, unless perhaps it might be a jellyfish, as could go floating past the guards like a swirl of sand and slip through a lobster's claws without wakin' up the lobster. Anyways, the long and the short of it was that all those sea creatures woke up one fine day and found they could no more breathe on land than what a pig can fly; and a rare old taking they were in. The jellyfish, he kept out of the way, but all the same he was too clever not to have thought of gettin' hold of someone as could let him know what was going on. That was why, when he was working the spell, he left one creature out of it, and that was his friend the turtle. So the turtle could still live out of the water if he'd a mind to, and the jellyfish was counting on him to let him know what happened in the sea king's palace, only the jellyfish was afraid to go back there himself, see?

What happened was that all the sea-beasts met together to think what was to be done. And in the end they sent to ask the advice of the Queen of Atlantis, her in the western country where the sun drops into the sea: and the old Queen, she told them that nothing would undo that spell without they could get the liver of a cat and each

and every one of them swim over it at a high tide and a full moon.

'All very well,' says the lord of the turbots to the rest of them, when they'd heard the Queen's advice, 'but cats in the sea's no more plentiful than bears on a 'bus. Where we going to find a cat, 'cept on dry land, where we can't catch him?'

'Ah, and ask him very kindly to let us have his liver,' says the king of the codfish, 'while he isn't usin' it, like. Strikes me we're in trouble.'

But then they remembers that there was one beast as could still help them, and that was the turtle. So they sent for him, and when he come they tells him to go up top and come back with a nice, healthy cat as they had a use for. And he give them his word as he wouldn't come back without 'en.

Well, the turtle, he swims up through the sea and goes all along the shore until he comes to a village. And what does he do then but he crawls up on to the beach not far from the houses and pretends as he's stranded 'there? Well, sure enough, after a time a cat, as belonged to a fisherman in one of the cottages, he catches sight of him and he thinks whatever's that? Cats are very inquisitive, you know, especially young ones, and in particular they can't leave anything alone if they sees it's moving about and acting like it's in trouble. So up comes the cat, jumping about all pop-eyed and putting out a paw to pat the turtle's shell and then the turtle's head. The turtle, he acts up helpless-like until he sees his chance, and then he suddenly grabs the cat's paw in his mouth, and drags him into the water, and off he goes.

All the way back the cat was hollerin' and strugglin' and makin' such a fuss that the turtle could hardly get along. So at last he tells him as there's nothing to worry about and he's just taking him down to be guest of honour at a big assembly in the sea king's hall. He promised him all manner of wonderful things and in the end the cat calmed down and sat quiet, although the turtle took good care to keep a-hold of his paw.

When the turtle arrived back, all the fishes and

other sea-creatures came crowding round, cheering and waving and making a great to-do, so that the cat came to believe that he really had been invited as a guest of honour. They made a great fuss of him and of course no one told him the rights of it at all. He was given ever such a good meal and settled down comfortably on a nice soft bed of sponges, and after a bit he went right off to sleep. And meanwhile all the sea-creatures agreed to meet again the next day and open him up for his liver. No, you needn't start crying, now, Miss Jean, 'cos this tale all ends up a lot different from what you're reckonin' it's going to.

Well, now, see, in the middle of the night the pussy-cat wakes up and there's this cold, rubbery thing a-ticklin' his nose and bumpin' up against his head and that. So he says, 'Who's there, and what do you want with me?' And the long and short of it was, it turns out to be that cunning old jellyfish, as had come to tell him what was what.

'They're going to cut you up,' he says, 'and take out your liver to make a charm with. That is, if you don't look sharp and come with me. I'm the one as wants to get you out of here.'

And with that he tries to take the cat on his back and swim away, same as the turtle. Only he was that soft and slippery, see, there wasn't nothing for the cat to hang on to. Dear oh law, didn't they just try it all ways, and the cat that scared with what the jellyfish had told him, he was hangin' on by his claws and tremblin' bad as a jelly himself. At last they had to give it up, and the jellyfish went off in a bad temper, thinking as that was the end of all his clever plans.

But cats are that artful, you never knows what they'll be up to next. It's no good you thinking you'll be ahead of a cat, 'cause he'll be off down the street while you're still lookin' up the chimney. When it come to breakfast time they brought him all sorts of nice things, same as what they had the night before, but he just sat there and wouldn't touch a bit of it.

'What's the matter?' asks the lord of the turbots, very civil – only they wanted him to eat a lot and go to sleep again, see, so's they could put him out nice and quiet and no trouble – 'Isn't it to your liking?'

'Oh yes, yes,' says the cat, acting very disappointed-like. 'You're very kind,' he says, 'but the truth is, I had a very bad night and it's all my own fault,' he says. 'I can't think how I can have been so stupid and forgetful.'

'Why, what you forgotten, then?' someone asks him.

'Well,' says the cat, 'I always washes my liver once a month – it's healthy, you know, for us land creatures: we all do it – and then I hangs it out to dry. And what with coming away so sudden yesterday afternoon, I clean forgot about it, and so of course that lovely dinner what you give me last night was bound to disagree with me. I really daren't eat no more,' he says. 'I feels wrong enough now.' And then he rolls about and acts up ever so well, so they all thinks he must a' been took real bad.

'Ennit proper real?' says the king of the codfish. 'Just our luck, eh?'

'Dear oh dear,' says the lord of the turbots, 'don't it always just about choose bank 'oliday to rain?' he says. 'Why'd that old turtle have to pick one without a liver? Lucky he told us. We might very well have had all our trouble for nothin'. Turtle'll just have to take him back to pick up his liver, and bring him down here again tonight,' he says.

So off they goes, the turtle and the pussy-cat, back up to the village by the sea. 'Course, as soon as they got there, Mr Pussy, he says, 'Oh good,' he says, 'there's my liver still hangin' out on the line. I won't be just a moment.' And off he went, and he took good care not to come back, too. The poor old turtle, he waited and waited, but at last he had to go home again and tell them as they'd all been made fools of.

And from that day to this, no cat will go into water or anywhere near it, not if he can help; 'cause that old pussy-cat told all the others and they've passed it on, mother to child, see? They're not giving the fish any more chances.

And no beast comes out of the sea on to the land, only 'cept for the jellyfish and the turtle – though as for turtles, I've never seen one meself and I'm only tellin' you what they told me. And as for the jellyfish, he goes floating about all by himself in the water, for none of the other creatures will have anything to do with him, and 'tain't surprisin', is it? He floats up on the beach when he feels like it, and then he waits to be washed off by the next tide. And if anyone touches him or interferes with him he stings them, because he's afraid they've come to punish him for all his mean tricks. But there's no doing anything about it now and he's best left alone, 'ceptin' you wants to be laid up bad.

There's the donkey-man come now, Master Richard, see him up there? One ride you can have, you and Miss Jean, the both of you. My goodness me, tuppence a go, prize for daylight robbery and they'd be sendin' that there donkey-man up to Lord Kitchener for a decoration, that they would. There you are, then, Master Richard, there's four coppers and just you take good care of 'em now. And mind you comes straight back here, where I'm sitting. Don't get wandering about, nor stood listening to that vulgar ventriloquialist or whatever he calls himself. You be a good boy and girl now, and I'll take you up to see the camrockskura 'safternoon. And *do* stop kicking your toes like that, Master Richard. Those sandals have got to last!

THE GIANT EEL

'Good day! Good day!' Well, monsieur, to tell you the truth, that's all the English I know, and I always say it to the American ladies and gentlemen that I take out fishing, because that's what they want to hear. I didn't know you were French. And monsieur speaks Polynesian – wonderful! Well, I'll speak Polynesian, and perhaps a dash of French as well, eh? Merveilleux! Ça marche bien.

Most of the tourists at the Club Med. are American, of course, with a few British now and again, but we do get French as well; and that's not surprising – Tahiti and Morea and the other islands being French, all the way west to Bora-Bora. Non, monsieur, je n'ai jamais été à Bora-Bora. I come from Raiatea myself – that's where I was born. I worked five years in Papeete, but this last three years I've been with the Club on Morea. Well, it's good money; et le travail, ce n'est pas trop dur. Yes, it's my own boat and I'm still paying for it, but the Club maintain it while I'm here; and buy the gas, of course. Good day!

Is monsieur a good sailor? I ask only because I think it's going to be choppy out in the lagoon, especially if we go beyond the big *motu* over there. You'd be surprised how many people are sick, even when it's calm. That's what I keep this bucket for!

Regardez, monsieur – non, par là, over your shoulder. From here you get a fine view of the mountain with the hole through the top. The only one in the world, they say. Non, non, c'est tout à fait naturel. Volcanic rock, voyez-vous. No, I've never been up there. The climb would be very hard – no path, and miles of thick forest, very steep. I never knew anyone who did it.

Monsieur is enjoying his holiday? Bien. Oh, yes, there's plenty going on. Monsieur Nat, Monsieur Big Luke et Monsieur Chrétien – they keep things moving. You swim much, monsieur? Oh, you've been down with the Scuba divers? I couldn't do that, now. I should be afraid. Who is your instructor? Oh, the young Dutchman, Monsieur Clement. He's very good with the beginners, they say. But a snorkel mask and flippers, that's enough for me. I can get down twenty-five feet with those and I don't want to go any lower. One sees a great deal like that. The fish are very beautiful, n'est-ce pas?

No, no sharks here, monsieur. Not inside the reef. You can be quite certain of that. You've seen a giant ray? In the distance – well, in the distance is the only way you're likely to see him. He's a great coward, you know. He lies in the sand on the bottom. If you were to tread on him, ah oui, vous seriez blessé, bien sur, but almost always he sees you and goes first. The stonefish? Well, they tell you the stonefish is deadly poisonous and I dare say that may be true, but they tell you merely so that it can't be said they

didn't warn you. I've never heard of anyone being stung by a stonefish. But they're ugly little brutes to look at, sure.

If you're out diving along the reef, monsieur, you may very well happen to see one of the great conger eels. Oh, you *did* see one? I hope you gave him a wide berth – well, no one but a fool would do anything else, would he? It's eerie, isn't it, the way he sticks his great, wicked, flat head out of a crevice and turns it this way and that to keep you in sight? Evil creatures – dangerous. All the same, it was the giant eel, long ago, who gave the Islands their greatest blessing. I dare say you know the tale. Without that gift, there wouldn't have been any life for man on the Islands – no, nor anywhere in the South Seas, come to that. They may call it an old woman's tale, but what I always say is, the world's a very old place, and we can't tell, can we, what may or may not have happened all those years ago? It doesn't follow, because things are the way they are now, that they've always been the same. The story goes back to the days of Maui – the hero Maui, that first fished up the Islands out of the ocean, and caught the sun in a noose to shine for ever. Without Maui there wouldn't be anything here at all – only just the sea. But then, without Te Tuna, men couldn't have lived on the Islands all these years. You don't know the tale of Te Tuna, monsieur? Well, if you'd like to hear it, I'll tell you. There's not many people tell the old stories now – not in Tahiti, anyway – but if you were to go and live on some of the smaller islands you'd hear them told – once they'd got to know you, that is.

Te Tuna, long ago – he was the giant eel of Orea; the most terrible creature in the sea. He was feared from the west to the east and back again. The sharks feared him, the rays and the great clams below the reefs – clams that can close on the arm of a strong young sponge diver and hold him pinned until he drowns. There's nothing breaks *their* grip. Any creature that aroused Te Tuna's anger he killed; either he himself or his merciless followers, for they could pursue faster than any swimming creature could

escape. His rage turned the sea dark and when he chose, his magic power could make the waves tower up and shatter the coral.

Sometimes he used to roam the deep ocean, searching out the dark places of his kingdom and making sure that all saw him and felt the terror of his presence. But at other times he lived at his ease, in his great sea palace of rock and black coral, far below the Islands. And from there he would send out his messengers and spies, to bring him news of all that was borne on the waves and winds: and his fighters too he would send out, whenever there was killing to be done.

Nevertheless, there was one who could sway Te Tuna and make use of his power as she pleased, and that was his consort, the beautiful Hina of the Sky. Many, many tales are told of Hina – more than I could remember and more than any Papahé has heard, that's certain. At one time she dwelt in the moon, and at another in the ice-cold mountains, where mortal men could see her glorious body flashing beneath the clouds of sunset. The pupils of her eyes were greenstone and her hair was like the long, crimson weed that streams back and downward when the white foam spills from the reefs. In love she was like the barracuda – his appetite knows no end. But at this time of which I speak, it pleased her to live with Te Tuna, both because of his power and might, and because of the strength of his desire for her, which consumed him whenever she chose to kindle it. That was often.

How long warm Hina lived with Te Tuna, in that dark palace under the waves, I can't tell – nor whether she bore him children – but at last there came, they say, a time when she grew weary of his love, and longed only for the sun's light and the embraces of a man. Yet Te Tuna himself remained no less full of longing and, because of his continual desire to be with her, went less often than before about the depths of the sea. And Hina – more beautiful and sly than any broad-loined girl of Taravao or Tautira – thought only how to be rid of him and go her way to some other bed.

Well, so it came about – so she brought it about – that one day, when he was lying spent beside her, she said, 'I will swim up to the Islands, my lord, and seek food to cook for you; the best that can be found. And on my return I will prepare a feast for you and your followers – fruit, pork, and sea crab; bananas and sweet potatoes.' And then Te Tuna, drowsy in his luxury, replied, 'Go, then, vahine, bright lightning that melts me, but see that thou returnest quickly, like the moon from behind a cloud.'

Then Hina swam, all naked, up through the waves; and when she came to the Islands she smelt the frangipani in the coolness before dawn. She was glad then. She swam through a gap in the reef and so in to where the fresh water flowed into the lagoon from the forest; and there she sat and wrung out her long hair, while the sun rose and shone upon her breasts.

By and by came the men, with their nets and paddles, to loose their canoes and go fishing, and she called to them, 'Who will lie with me? Who will be the first to take me in his arms beside the water? For I burn!'

They looked at her and knew her who she was, warm Hina of the Sky, the girl all golden, like a candle-bush tree in the morning. They trembled and grew big for her – they were men, monsieur, like you and me. And then they thought of Te Tuna and recalled the appearance, when he had finished with them, of those who had displeased him: and one of them called out, 'Why do you torment us, Hina? We see you, and we also know your lord, him who commands the tidal wave and the typhoon. Leave us in peace. Go and ease your desire elsewhere.' Then Hina swam away, weeping.

She swam to Morea and to Fakarava, to Huahine and to the green hills of sacred Raiatea. She spread her glowing thighs in the green glades and called to the young men, 'Take me! Melt upon me! My breasts are swollen! I cannot bear my longing!' And they replied, 'Neither can we! Will you first drive us mad and then bring down the vengeance of Te Tuna upon our village?' They fled to spend themselves upon their own girls, that they might the better resist Hina with the crimson hibiscus in her hair. But they could no more drive her from their inward thoughts than one can drive the scent of jasmine from the darkness. Monsieur has suffered this pain? Alors, on n'a besoin d'en parler plus.

So at last she came to Bora-Bora. That's a little island, a long way down-wind, where a high, flat-topped mountain, like a round tower, stands above a village beside the lagoon; and a big *motu* lies between the village and the reef. Monsieur has been there? C'est juste? Bien. At that time, long ago, Maui was living on Bora with his mother, Hua-Hega – the hero Maui Tiki-Tiki a Taranga; he who first devised the barbed fish-hook and the eel-trap, who created the dog for man, and played tricks on the gods themselves; Maui the bringer of fire.

Maui had come from fishing and was spreading his net to dry between the corner-posts of his hut, when he heard the calling of warm Hina on the shore. He laid by his net and went towards her, and as she raised her arms he felt his loins like the shadow of a hill when the sun sinks behind it. Yet as he recognized her even Maui knew fear, to think of Te Tuna and the staring pupils of his white, lidless eyes. He tried to cover himself – for he was naked – and she, perceiving the malady from which he suffered, laughed and swayed her hips, to provoke him, if she could, beyond endurance.

Perhaps even Maui would have fled like the rest – Maui Tiki-Tiki a Taranga, fisher-up of islands – had not his mother, coming softly behind him, whispered in his ear, 'Take the woman. Take her for yourself, my son, and have no fear. It is destiny, and a part of the gods' ordering of the world, that she should be yours. Yet only the gods know what plant is ordained to spring from this seed.'

So Maui took her, and she lived with him on Bora-Bora. He was her fisherman and she cooked the food he brought her. In her lagoon he cast his hook. She grew fruit in the forest glade, and he

plucked that fruit and ate. She showed him a warm stream above a leafy cascade, and he bathed in that pool. Often, at nightfall, the wind blew and the trees tossed and tumbled together, but before the moon had reached the zenith they were still; and then the branches lay tranquil all night until sunrise.

They say it's the wind that carries tidings through the Islands, for nothing else could bear them so fast. Every creature throughout the ocean could smell on that breeze the frangipani and tiaré blossom of Hina's love, for from Bora it blew above the waves and beneath the waves; and soon it was stirring even the long, black weed about the door of Te Tuna's palace. There was none that dared to tell him; but he caught the scent himself, they say, and writhed upon the coral as though he had been burned with a glowing branch. He broke the rocks about his throne, yet did not know that he had done so. For a whole day he spoke no word and none dared speak to him. Then he called for his four chief followers, and they, rising up with him through the seas, set off for Bora. I'm glad I didn't meet them on the way.

They reached the island at dawn, coming from the east, five of them swimming together into the surf. As they neared, a hurricane swept across the island, bending the trees flat and tearing them so that the whole place became a dark, pelting turmoil, a storm of leaves and sand. And behind the wind followed the tidal wave – a great curve of water that seemed to be carrying the clouds on top of it. Riding on that wave came Te Tuna and his warriors, each racing to be the first to sink his fangs into Maui's body. It broke the reef, smashing it as though it were no more than a clay pot: they say you can see the gap to this day. Te Tuna, rearing out of the sea, half as high as the hills, burst through the reef with fragments of jagged coral sticking to his flanks.

Just as the sun rose, that great wave came rushing across the breadth of the lagoon, rolling over the *motu* as though there were no *motu* there. And the first rays, slanting all across the sea, showed Maui standing naked on the beach, calm and ready, only his hair streaming in that terrible wind. As he raised his hand – that trickster's hand that fashioned the first fish-hook and stole the fire – the wave curled over, all along its green length, and went sliding down and back towards the ocean. The whole lagoon was drawn after it until the coral itself lay bare, the long weeds and the coloured anemones on the rocks. And upon that bitter coral Te Tuna and his followers were thrown down and torn.

Three died then and there, and their bodies lay bleeding on the bed of the lagoon, enough almost to fill it up again: Pupu-vai-e-noa, he that slew the seven blue sharks beyond Fatu-Hiva and threw their bodies on the shore for the crabs and gulls; Porporo-tu-huaga, who loved the chief's daughter of Rimatara and carried her away by night, guiding himself by the taulapa, the phosphorescence that flashes deep below the long swell and always aligns itself in the direction of the nearest land; and Naga-vai-i-e-rire, who broke the net of Nakaa on the north point of Butaritari and on that account believed himself immortal. Carrion they became that day, one and all. Only the last of those four escaped – Toke-a-kura, the swift swimmer, the long-fanged, he that tore out the great blow-hole below the rocks of Tahiti and strewed the fragments from Hauru to Terurua. Wounded as he was, he fled to the broken reef, crawled through it and plunged to safety in the ocean beyond.

So Te Tuna was left alone, and Maui could have slain him then and there. Yet he did not; partly, perhaps, because he did not know how to go safely about such a task; and again, it may be, because he thought to humiliate Te Tuna by showing him defeated to warm Hina of the Sky, that she might lose all desire that ever she might have felt to return to him and his palace under the sea. Whatever Maui's thoughts may have been, the tale tells only how, as the sea returned to fill the lagoon once more, he raised Te Tuna up and took him to his dwelling.

And here for a time Te Tuna lived, for the

truth was that he had no stomach to return to the deep ocean without his followers, to hear others whisper behind his back the tale of his defeat and to wonder how long they would now endure his rule. What words he spoke to Hina or she to him, and what were his thoughts as he saw her rise from Maui's bed to cook Maui's food – these things I never heard told. But one evening, they say, he burst out in loud anger and desperation, calling Maui a coward and a deceiving, treacherous thief who had no courage to lay aside his tricks and magic and fight face to face to the death, his power against his enemy's. And with that, just as night was falling, the two of them went down to the shore.

Maui stood on the sand, close above the water-line, and Te Tuna wreathed and swayed about him, seeking to terrify him and to weaken and destroy his courage for the contest. Yet he showed no sign of fear, not even when Te Tuna at last commenced the struggle upon which they had agreed; shrunk himself, contracting and diminishing, and vanished into Maui's body, to destroy him, if he could, from within.

All that night, as Te Tuna wound his hidden course, Maui stood motionless beside the lagoon. The moon rose, passed across the sky and sank once more into the sea, while the spiders and land crabs went scuttling about their dark business. The breeze from the forest carried along the shore the rustling of leaves and the pattering of the waterfalls, but Maui – he made no sound, his feet in the sand broad and flat as baking-stones in a fire. What he endured, as the terrible Orea eel strove to destroy him, none can say. The sun rose again and climbed towards noon, but still Maui never stirred and gave no sign of the combat within, silent and deadly as a battle of great fish in depths below daylight. And at last, just when it seemed that he could no longer endure, Te Tuna reappeared in his true shape, for against Maui he could not prevail.

And now Maui made short work of what was left to do. Hardly had he, in his turn, vanished into Te Tuna's body, than the giant eel fell writhing on the sand. His great fangs gaped wide in agony and then, his body torn apart like an old garment, he died without a word.

Maui cut off the head for a trophy and carried it back to his dwelling. Yet Hina, moved perhaps by pity for the death of him who had been her lover, would not suffer it to be displayed or mocked, so that night Maui buried it in the ground outside their door. As for the body on the sand, the land crabs had taken all before next dawn.

Now nothing was left to threaten Maui's peace, and he and Hina lived at their ease on Bora, secure in their delight and pleasure, looking no further and heedless of all else: so that as the months passed, they gradually forgot Te Tuna and the conflict in which he had died for love of the girl he lost to Maui. It may have been five, six – seven months after Te Tuna's death – it matters little how long – when one night Maui, emptied yet again into Hina's glowing loins, was lying at peace, listening to the distant surf on the reef and idly watching the moonlight moving across the ground outside the doorway. And there, as he gazed, he suddenly perceived a long, green shoot newly sprung from the ground – a shoot already putting forth leaves of a kind unknown to him. Then he remembered the buried head and he was afraid, for he could not tell what this might portend. Hina had fallen asleep, and he left her side and sought Hua-Hega, the wise woman his mother.

Now Hua-Hega had known in her heart all that had been ordained; all that was destined even before Hina first came to Te Tuna in the palace under the sea. This was why she had counselled Maui to take Hina for himself. And now, as they stood together beside that strange, sea-green frond sprung from the head of his defeated enemy, she made him swear to tend and nurture it as the most precious thing in all the Islands.

'This,' said she, 'is nothing less than the divine gift of him who once hated you, but who is now set free from the sorrow and bitter torment of love. This is the token of his blessing and forgiveness, which we must accept in humble gratitude, for it will be the staple of the Isles for evermore.'

This is that tree, monsieur, by which the Islands live – the coconut palm. Without the palm there would be no men and women in all the ocean, for it is the most bountiful tree in the world. From the fruit we get both food and drink. The wood makes logs and planks, both for dwellings and canoes. The leaves we dry and use for thatch, the scooped-out shells form our eating and drinking vessels. Even the fibrous growth beneath the fruit is of use to our women for wrappings and cleaning-rags. Such was Te Tuna's gift, the immortal husk of sea-green, bestowed by a sea-king in token of his forgiveness of Maui Tiki-Tiki a Taranga. Yet as every child knows, it was Maui who caused it to flourish, and later to spread throughout all the islands.

Well, monsieur, unless the tale makes up for the catch, I was wrong and it's not a good day, for we've hooked nothing, lost nothing and even seen nothing. Shall I take her back to the jetty? At four o'clock Monsieur Big Luke will be taking out the Scuba divers, and we can be back by a quarter to. That, sans doute, will be your best chance of seeing fish this afternoon. Or you might sit in the shade and watch Mademoiselle Renée on the volley-ball court. Perhaps Maui himself would regret that he never had the chance to do that?

MICE IN THE CORN

Now will everybody please come here, keep quiet and listen to me! Toby, that includes you! We've arrived early, which is much better than arriving late, and it will be half an hour before Mr Britten is ready for us in the hall. All those over eleven can go outside, if they like, and walk about, but will you – I didn't say you could go yet! Sonia, Marie-Thérèse, will you please wait until I've finished! Hilary Ann, come back here! Now, will you all remember that you are at The Maltings, that you are the Finchley Children's Music Group and that we are Mr Britten's guests? You must behave properly and not mess about or do anything to get the Group a bad name at Snape. Is that clear – you, David, and Melanie? Anyone who gets into any sort of mischief will *not* take part in the concert. All right, off you go. And you are *not* to go wandering off down the marshes, do you understand? You're to be back here punctually in half an hour, and Poll will be waiting for you in the next room.

The rest of you, sit down here. Anyone who wants lemonade can tell Poll now and she'll go and get enough for everyone. Toby, will you *please* stop pulling Susan's hair this minute? Now, who's going to tell us a story? Juliet? Philip? Well, somebody; come along!

What? You think *I* ought to tell a story? Not fair unless I'm counted in too, Priscilla, did you say? Well, I suppose – let me see. If I *do* tell a story, I insist on proper attention, because it will certainly be one that nobody's heard before. Er – yes – I'll tell you a very old story, about the mice in the corn. No, Rosamond, it's nothing at all to do with Bishop Hatto. It's a great deal older than that, and it all happened in Wales a very long time ago.

Once upon a time there were two Welsh chieftains, the Lord of Dyfed and his young stepson, Pryderi the Generous, who were returning home from a war which they had fought in England. The fighting had been successful, and they'd made certain that no one from England would dare to attack them for a long time to come. All the same, they weren't feeling entirely happy about the future, because during the campaign they had both quarrelled bitterly with another chief on their own side – a man named Lloyd the Enchanter, who had become so angry with them that he had gone home, taking all his warriors with him and leaving Pryderi and the Lord of Dyfed to fight the English by themselves. Lloyd wasn't much of a warrior, but he was known to be a great and powerful wizard, and both the old and the young prince felt troubled at the thought that he might very well be plotting his revenge upon them.

As the two chiefs, with their warriors, rode up to their castle, which was called Arberth, their

wives were waiting at the gate to welcome them with garlands, and silver goblets of wine on a gold tray: and all the servants and tenants sang a song of welcome, accompanied by a harper who was almost as good as Mr Osian Ellis. The Welsh have always been great singers, as I dare say you know, and the harper had made up this song for the occasion and rehearsed the tenants very well, so that none of the altos strained the tone at all, *Sheila*. No, I've no idea what it was called, but it certainly *wasn't* '"Bang, bang, bang", said the nails in the ark.' The Lord of Dyfed's wife was called Riannon, and Pryderi's wife, who was quite young – not much older than some of you – was called Cigfa.

The next day, the two chiefs gave a great feast to all their warriors and tenants, and there was any amount for everybody to eat and drink. In those days they always used to end the fighting before early autumn if they possibly could, partly because the men had to be home to get the harvest in and partly because there were no proper roads or ways of protecting soldiers against bad weather, so that it was more or less impossible to keep an army in the field during the winter. And before the hard weather they generally used to kill quite a lot of their cattle, because it was difficult to keep more than a few of them properly fed right through until the next spring. Most of the meat was salted down in tubs, to last them through the winter, but with part of it they used to have a feast – the last fresh meat most people were going to get for several months.

The chiefs and their wives feasted first, together with their most important household officers and soldiers. When they'd finished, they left the hall and the feasting began among the pages, squires and servants. Then, as the weather was fine and the afternoon air cool and pleasant, the Lord of Dyfed, together with Pryderi and their two wives, walked out through the fields

and up a green hill near-by – the Gorsedd Arberth.

Now while they were standing on the Gorsedd Arberth, looking out over their fields and flocks and barns below, and the smoke of the dwellings beyond, they were suddenly dazzled by a great flash, like lightning, after which there followed immediately a tremendous roll of thunder. Then, as the two chieftains clasped their frightened ladies in their arms to reassure and encourage them, there fell over the hill-top a mist so thick that they couldn't see even the rocks nearest them.

At this all four felt a deep fear and misgiving. It was silent in the mist and they couldn't hear a sound from below – no lowing of cattle and no shouts or blowing of horns from the castle. Groping, they stumbled their way down the hill and then followed the course of a little brook which they knew flowed into the castle moat. But the castle, when they reached it, was nothing but a smoking ruin; and not a voice, either human or animal, answered them from among its fallen beams and stones. Together they clambered over the shattered gateway and searched everywhere, but dared not separate, not only because of the mist and gathering darkness, but also because of their terror of what might still happen. They searched for more than an hour, but the only living creatures they could find were the Lord of Dyfed's hounds. At last they took shelter, as best they could, in the ruins of the armoury, where part of the roof, which was still standing, kept out the cold rain that had begun to fall.

'This is Lloyd the Enchanter's work,' said the lady Riannon at length. 'It is his evil power which has destroyed our peace and prosperity. Nonetheless, I myself believe that, although he has done us this mischief, God's greater power and wisdom has not allowed him to kill either our people or our beasts and cattle. We haven't found a single dead body. Therefore I believe that Lloyd has not been able to kill them, but has spirited them away to some secret place of his own.'

'Here at least are some weapons left,' said the Lord of Dyfed. 'I will fight Lloyd and by some means or other contrive to save our people and recover the kingdom.'

'But how can you fight him?' answered Riannon. 'He's not here to be fought – there's only this mist and darkness. We don't know where to look for him; and worse still, we have nothing to eat.'

So at length, driven by hunger and want, they took the hounds and wandered away across country, through all the Seven Cantrefs of Dyfed; and wherever they went they found the land waste and desolate.

Just a minute. Sheila, is that someone at the door? Good afternoon. Are you looking for me? I beg your pardon – what did you say? No, I'm sorry, I'm afraid we can't move out of here for about twenty minutes. Well, I'm afraid you must have made a mistake. Yes, I'm Mrs Andrewes of the Finchley Children's Music Group, and I have to keep these children together in one place until Mr Britten is ready for them. It won't be very long, but we can't move just at the moment. Thank you.

Soon the two chieftains and their poor wives were reduced to great want and distress. For a time they hunted and fished for food, but as the winter came on harder they made their way into England and here, where there was no one to recognize them, they worked in the towns – in Shrewsbury, I dare say, and perhaps in Chester and Ludlow too. It was hard work, for people who'd been lords and ladies, to make things like saddles, arrows and boots with tools and their bare hands, and all the time they were homesick for their own country; so when the summer returned they went back to the Seven Cantrefs, resolving to stay there, and to try to rest content with living and hunting in the wild.

Now one day, when the two chiefs were in the woods, their hounds started a big, white boar which led them on until at last it went plunging into a dark thicket. They were following it cautiously when all of a sudden, coming to a clearing, they saw in front of them a dark, ivy-covered tower: and through the open door of this tower the boar ran, and the hounds after it. Pryderi was just going to follow them in, when the Lord of Dyfed caught his arm.

'There's some great danger in there, my son,' he said. 'I can sense it. Whatever you do, don't go in!'

'Don't try to stop me!' cried Pryderi. 'If one of us doesn't go in after them we shall lose our hounds. The boar may well have turned at bay already; or it may have made its way out through some hole on the far side, and the hounds will follow it before we can find the line.'

'Better to lose the hounds than our lives!' said the Lord of Dyfed.

But Pryderi broke away from him, ran forward and disappeared through the doorway. No sooner had he done so than all became as silent as midnight; no cry of hounds, and no answer when the Lord of Dyfed called his name. The lord waited a long time but at last, as night was falling, he was forced to give his step-son up for lost, and returned to the ruins of Arberth with the heaviest heart he had ever borne.

When Riannon heard his evil news, she was stricken with grief even deeper than her husband's, and blamed him bitterly for the loss of her son. He had no spirit to answer her, for he too felt himself to blame.

'I should have drawn my sword on him,' said he, 'before I let him enter that place.'

That night, as the lord lay exhausted and asleep, Riannon rose quietly and slipped out by herself into the woods. The moon was bright and she was able to follow the track which the boar had trampled over the soft earth and fallen leaves. And so she too came to the thicket and, entering it, saw before her the dark tower.

The door was still standing open and she called Pryderi by name, but there was no answer and at last, though very much afraid, she ventured in.

As soon as she had passed through the arch she saw, in the middle of the moonlit courtyard,

her son standing quite still beside a marble fountain basin, on the rim of which rested a golden bowl fastened with four gold chains. His right hand lay on the bowl and she could see that he was in a trance, unable to move or speak. At the sight of him standing there, before her very eyes, unseeing and speechless though she, his own mother, was stretching out her arms to him and calling him by name, she grew beside herself and, without thinking of what might come about if she too touched the bowl, she tried to move it away from him. On the instant the moon was dimmed, there came a roll of thunder like the one which had dazed them on the hill a year before, and then tower, mother and son vanished like ghosts into the darkness.

So the Lord of Dyfed and poor young Cigfa were left alone, the one robbed of his wife and the other of her husband. And this was the worst hardship and sorrow they underwent in all their lives. Not even the hounds were left them to hunt with and it seemed as though they must starve. In desperation, the Lord of Dyfed tramped many miles to the house of a farmer beyond the boundaries of the Seven Cantrefs and from him begged a load of seed corn, promising to repay it at harvest time. Then, humbling himself to the work of a peasant, he cleared and dug three little fields and sowed them with the corn.

In this at least it seemed that they might have a gleam of luck at last, for the corn came up thick and green and, as it ripened, swelled large in the ear. At last it was ready for reaping and one morning the Lord of Dyfed rose early, planning to spend a long day in harvesting.

But when he came to the first field, he found all his corn stripped to the straw and the whole field bare. Not a single ear of corn was left; and yet there was not a mark on the ground – no sign of a reaper, no tracks of a cart or any path trodden through the straw. He searched all about, could find nothing to show how this robbery might have been carried out.

The following morning the second field was as bare as the first, and now the Lord of Dyfed began to feel afraid, for he knew that this disaster meant nothing less than their death by starvation.

'This must be the last stroke of Lloyd's revenge,' he said to Cigfa. 'Well, he's tormented us long enough and never dared to show his face in fair fight: soon he'll be able to rest content with our death. But at least I'll go down fighting as best I can. I'll keep watch tonight and find out by what evil means he has done this work.'

So that night the Lord of Dyfed hid himself among the bushes on the edge of the third and last field. And about midnight he heard a pattering like approaching rain, a rustling along the ground and a sound of squeaking coming nearer and nearer. As he peered about in the moonlight, he suddenly realized that his field was being attacked by an army – an army of mice! Into the corn they came, nibbling and tugging, pulling down and devouring his harvest, stalk by stalk and ear by ear. He stared aghast and his drawn sword fell from his hand, for how could he fight against such an attack as this? Yet as he watched, rage overcame him and, hardly knowing what he was doing, he plunged forward and made a snatch at the nearest mouse – a particularly large, sleek one that seemed to be directing the others. It turned to run, but it was slow and clumsy and he caught it before it could escape.

At first he had the idea that this might perhaps be Lloyd himself, transformed to a mouse by his magic arts. He taunted it and dared it to resume human shape and fight him. But soon he gave up this hope, for to start with it was a female mouse; and besides, the others, who were so many that they could easily have attacked him, made no attempt to save it, but finished their wicked work and departed as they had come.

The Lord of Dyfed tied up the mouse in his glove and, returning to the ruins of Arberth, sat until dawn beside the cold hearth. Soon afterwards Cigfa woke and, when she saw the glove hanging on a nail with the string tied round it, asked him what this might mean.

'We're ruined and undone,' said he. 'But at least I've caught one of the thieves and as God's my judge I'll hang her this morning!'

'Hang a mouse?' replied Cigfa. 'Dear father, I fear our sufferings must have driven you from your own good sense. Even our wretched death will seem nothing but ridiculous if such a tale is told in years to come. They'll say you lost even your wits at the last. For the once-great Lord of Dyfed to play such a foolish game as hanging a mouse! Suppose someone should see you? Have you no pride left?'

'No one will see me,' replied the Lord of Dyfed grimly. 'For these last two years, as well you know, there has been no traveller through this ruined land of ours. But still there is law; and I mean to enforce it.'

Soon after, when the sun had risen higher, the lord went out and cut two small forked sticks, and then a third stick for a cross-bar.

'I shall hang her,' said he to Cigfa, 'at the summit of the Gorsedd Arberth – that very place where Lloyd's evil deeds first struck us down. Lend me that fine silken lace from your bodice. It will do well enough for a rope.'

So, taking the glove with his prisoner in it, he once again climbed the Gorsedd Arberth, and on its top set up the gallows, driving the forked sticks firmly into the ground and fastening the bar between them. But then, rising from his knees and happening to look down the hill, he was astonished to see, climbing the slope below, a wayfarer – one who looked as though he might be an old pedlar, or perhaps a tinker or carpenter tramping in search of work. The man came up the hill to the summit, greeted him and sat down on the grass.

'Why,' said he, staring first at the Lord of Dyfed and then at the tiny gallows and the tied-up glove, 'may I ask what work this is that you're setting about on this fine morning?'

'I'm executing a thief,' replied the Lord of Dyfed. 'A mouse that's devoured my corn.'

'Why,' said the traveller, laughing, 'I'd say that would be a more proper job for your cat!

You look like a man who's seen better days, too. Why stoop to such foolishness, even though you may be down on your luck?'

'You attend to your business,' answered the Lord of Dyfed, 'and I'll attend to mine.'

'Do you know,' said the stranger, 'I don't think you can be quite yourself, and I've a mind to save you from such unbecoming nonsense, which you'd be certain to regret later on. So if you like I'll give you sixpence for the mouse.'

'Keep your sixpence!' replied the Lord of Dyfed, 'and let me be.' So the wayfarer shrugged his shoulders and went on his way.

But the lord wasn't left uninterrupted long enough to finish his task, for hardly had his first visitor gone than he saw another coming – this time a priest riding on an old horse. The priest dismounted at the top of the hill and then, staring at the gallows, asked, just like the first man, what was going on. The Lord of Dyfed told him.

'You know,' said the priest, 'I don't care for that at all, somehow, and I'll tell you why. I think it's distasteful, and even blasphemous in a way, for I myself have attended condemned men to the gallows before now, and it's a solemn business and nothing to make fun of. In fact, I feel so strongly about it that I'll give you a pound to drop the idea and let the mouse go. Do you agree?'

'No; and not for twenty either,' answered the Lord of Dyfed. 'If you don't like my notions, you can just be on your way, for I'm still lord in these parts.'

So the priest went off as the pedlar-man had done, and once more the Lord of Dyfed set to his work. He took the mouse out of the glove and had just tied the silk thread in a slip-knot round her neck when he heard a trampling of hooves on the turf below. Looking down for the third time, he was astonished to see a line of horsemen and mules wending their way among the gorse. At their head rode a dignified, white-haired old man in the mitre and robes of a bishop.

Now by this time the Lord of Dyfed felt thoroughly suspicious, for as he had said to Cigfa, not a single stranger had passed that way for two summers and more. So as the procession came up to the top of the hill, he held the mouse up in his hand and looked the bishop squarely in the eye.

'If you've come to ransom this mouse,' he said, 'forget it!'

'I have, as a matter of fact,' replied the bishop courteously. 'I happened to meet one of my priests coming down the hill – I'm just passing through, you know, on my way to Aberystwyth – and he told me what was going on. A man like you – you're the ruined Lord of Dyfed, are you not? – should certainly not be handling so worthless a creature! It will be very bad for the image of the ruling classes if news of this absurd matter should spread among the poor. Since you're so obstinate – or so my priest tells me – I'll pay you fifty pounds and we'll consider the thing concluded, shall we?'

'Certainly not!' answered the Lord of Dyfed. 'And now will you kindly –'

'Well,' said the bishop, 'I know you're a penniless man and no doubt that's why you're driving a hard bargain. You'd better name your own price.'

Then the Lord of Dyfed, still clutching the mouse tightly, said, 'Yes, Master Lloyd, I will. The price is two lives – my wife Riannon's and her son Pryderi's. You must return them here safe and sound.'

'Well, then, I will,' muttered the enchanter. 'And now give me the mouse.'

'Not yet,' continued the Lord of Dyfed. 'Next, you must restore the inhabitants, the cattle and all the prosperity of the Seven Cantrefs of Dyfed.'

'Yes, yes,' cried Lloyd – for the mouse, gripped between the lord's fingers, looked ready to choke. 'I'll see to all that!'

'*And* another thing,' said the Lord of Dyfed, leaning back comfortably against a rock. 'Who is this mouse? She seems very valuable. What was she doing in my cornfield?'

'She's my wife, curse you!' cried Lloyd. 'My people, all changed by my enchantments to mice, I sent to destroy your last hope of survival. Two fields they destroyed, and on the evening when they were setting out to devour the third, my wife and her ladies asked me to transform them too, so that they could join in the sport. But she is with child and went heavily, and that's why you caught her. Now, is that enough for you? Give her back to me, and all you have lost shall be returned!'

'Very well,' said the Lord of Dyfed. 'But I know you, Lloyd, and your cunning ways. So will you kindly get off that horse, kneel down here and swear on my sword never to trouble me or mine again, or seek to do us any ill whatsoever?'

'Ah!' shouted Lloyd. 'It's well for you, Lord of Dyfed, that you remembered that! Else I would have had my wife and my vengeance too.'

'No doubt,' answered the Lord of Dyfed. 'Well, here is your wife. But before I release her, I would like to see my own. And while you're about it, kindly bring the Lady Cigfa here as well.'

On the instant, he found the young prince Pryderi and the two ladies standing beside him. Looking down into the vale below, he could see his flocks and herds and horses, and beyond, the castle of Arberth, with banners flying and chimneys smoking in the light of the westering sun. Putting the mouse on the ground, he embraced his dear wife, but as he dried his tears and looked once more about him, he could see no sign of Lloyd or any of his retinue.

'I must have fallen asleep here, on the hill-top,' said Riannon, 'and a strange and evil dream it was that I suffered! We must already have stayed too long, for your soldiers will be expecting our return before the end of their feast. Why, whatever are those funny little sticks there, driven into the turf?'

So then the Lord of Dyfed – Oh, hullo, Ben! How nice of you to come round for us yourself! Yes, we're all quite ready. These are the juniors, and Poll's got the seniors waiting next door. Do you want us in the concert hall now? We won't be two minutes. Toby, will you please give Deirdre back her shoe *at once*? Everybody outside, *quietly*!

—THE MODDEY DHOO—

There you are, sir: a Guinness, and a gin-and-tonic for the lady, with ice and lemon. I hope she'll find it up to Washington standards. Oh, thank you very much, sir, that's very kind of you. I'll have a half of draught bitter. We look after our draught beer properly here, you know, and it's very good. Well, I can understand you might find it takes a little while to get a taste for British draught beer. Most American visitors say that. Myself, I wouldn't like iced beer, except in very hot weather, perhaps. Ah, I know what you're going to say – 'We don't get much of that over here, either'. Well, I dare say we don't. But you get more of the true flavour of the beer if it isn't ice-cold, you know; and then again, there's plenty of lads likes to drink a good many pints in an evening, and they could never do that if it was ice-cold, you know. 'Twould go to the stomach something terrible, wouldn't it? So it's good for trade, is our way of serving beer.

Yes, it *is* quiet just now – the season's hardly started, you see. But there'll be plenty coming in all through the summer, beginning in about four weeks' time. Holiday trade – plenty of that from May to September, both in Douglas and Peel: well, and all over the Island, really. It's grown a great deal over the last hundred years, I'm told. 'Tisn't surprising. First steamships and then aeroplanes, you see, bringing them in. Before

that, of course, the Isle of Man must have been a real lonely spot, stuck right out in the sea here, and a long sail both from England and Ireland too.

It's still a very funny place in some ways, you know, sir, is the Isle of Man. There's strange tales and strange beliefs still very much alive here, and plenty of people that take them seriously. For example, you must never talk about R-A-T-S on the Island. It's extremely unlucky, is that. You must call them 'the long-tails', or 'the fur-and-whiskers' or whatever you like, but never the R-A-T-S. You should hear some of the lads talking right here, in this very room, sometimes – specially on winter nights, when there's no visitors to the Island and they know there's none but themselves to hear – barring me, of course. Well, I'm not Manx-born, you see, though it's a great many years now I've been here – came over as a young man, and married a Manx girl too. So I'm all right, as far as they're concerned, though sometimes I can tell they reckon I'm still just a bit different from themselves, even now.

I haven't always had this place – only about ten years. It's a very nice little pub, is this; very snug in winter, when we get really cold winds from the west. I saw you having a look at the pictures on the walls. No, sir, I'm afraid I couldn't sell you any of them. They go with the place, you see, but apart from that, I wouldn't want to. That one of the Isle of Man Steam Packet leaving Douglas Bay – that's a beauty, isn't it? No, I really couldn't say why the pub's called 'The White House'. When you get back home you'll be able to tell them you've had a drink in the White House, won't you? There might be better company sometimes in this one than what there is in yours, I dare say, and maybe more honesty too, for the matter of that. Just my joke, you know, sir. There's not a great many American visitors come to the Island, actually: it's a bit off the beaten track, I suppose, though there's a deal of old stuff to be seen here; very old, some of it – and unique, too.

There's a lot of things either 'black' or 'white' on the Island, actually. You've noticed they put the names of the streets and other places up in Manx Gaelic as well as in English? Well, you'll see the word 'dhoo' quite often – that's 'black', you know. About two miles out of Peel, up the Kirk Michael road, you'll come to Lhergy Dhoo – where that writer's gone to live, what's his name, Mr Adams, who wrote that *Watership Down* – not that I've bothered to read it myself. 'Lhergy Dhoo' – that means 'the black hillside'. And then there's the Moddey Dhoo, of course, as you'll have heard of already, for sure.

What, they haven't told you about the Moddey Dhoo? Not up at Peel Castle they didn't? Well, I'm surprised at that, but very likely they didn't want to frighten you, or perhaps didn't want to frighten your lady, more like. No, madam, I'm sure you wouldn't be frightened, but then I'm not Manx, you see, any more than you are. They'd feel they didn't want to frighten you because they're very much afraid themselves, most of them – of the Moddey Dhoo, they are, anyhow – so they'd suppose you would be, you see. They wouldn't spend a night in the castle, not one of them.

Well, I'll tell you as much as I know, though I dare say there's some could tell you more – if you could get them to. 'Moddey Dhoo' means 'black dog', but all the same, the Moddey Dhoo's a lot more than just a black dog.

Yes, indeed, the castle *is* a wonderful old place – what's left of it, that is. But that's only the ghost, you might say, of what's been in times past. The Island wasn't Christianized from England, you know. No, it was Christianized from Ireland, by monks of St Patrick, a good forty years before ever St Augustine landed in England. And I dare say those old monks might have found some odd things when they landed in what was still an isolated, heathen country, don't you? Anyway, that's where they landed, where the castle is now, and it's called 'St Patrick's Isle' to this day.

There's been a castle of some kind or another on that site these fifteen hundred years. Before the causeway and the road were made – and that wasn't very long ago – that was a tidal island, you see; cut off at high tide, but having a harbour of its own in that bay on the south side, to say nothing of the little anchorage on the west, below what they call the Fenella Tower. You saw that? You couldn't get a modern boat in there, of course, but it was big enough for the boats of those old days. That tall, round tower is one of the very few buildings still left standing in the British Isles that was built before the Norman conquest. They call it the Tower of Refuge, because when the monks saw the Vikings' ships coming, they used to grab the Communion plate and hide up the tower. There's no proper doorway, as you probably saw – only an opening about ten feet up. Nor there's no stairs inside. It must have been all ladders, either wooden or rope. But the tower wouldn't burn, you see. They'd be all right up there.

The present castle walls you saw aren't very old, actually – somewhere between five and six hundred years. That's not old. But in those later days, of course, the place would have been full of soldiers, not monks. And it was soldiers that first saw the Moddey Dhoo, so the story goes. I don't know just exactly how long ago, but 'twas at night – one stormy winter's night, with the waves fairly crashing over the rocks below the

castle, and the soldiers of the guard glad enough to sit by the fire in the guard-room and no one particularly looking forward to his turn to go out on sentry, I dare say.

You saw the guard-room, sir, I take it, when you were up there? It's in the thickness of the gateway, beside the stairs and just inside the big door. Well, the story goes that as they were all in there by the fire, suddenly one of them turns round and what does he see come in but a great, black dog? It was huge; big as a calf, all black, with great eyes staring wide, that looked as though they were alight. Now, as I dare say you know, sir, in the normal way there's no animal can return a human being's gaze. They always turn away quite soon, and that's one method those lion-tamers use, I've been told, to gain authority over their beasts and dominate them. But this great dog, it stood and looked at those soldiers, and there wasn't one of them could meet its eyes. Every man looked somewhere else; and then the guard commander, he gets up and laid a-hold of his sword – or might have been his spear, or even his gun, for all I know – and he was going to go for the dog, to turn it out. But one of the soldiers caught his arm without a word and just pointed to it. It hadn't moved, but all the same it didn't take the guard commander more than a moment to see what the soldier meant. For the dog made never the least sound, and for all it was such a wet, cold night, there was never a bit of steam or vapour of breath out of its muzzle. Its great, shaggy coat was dry as a bone, and its paws had left no wet marks or mud at all on the floor. So after a few moments the guard commander put down his weapon and sat still.

The dog was between the soldiers and the door, and there was nobody cared to pass it. For a time they all just sat and looked at it, and couldn't even find any words to speak to each other. Then, after a while, the dog went and lay down in a corner; and there it stayed. They began talking again, but in low voices and very much aware of not being by themselves, as you might say. Then it came time to change the sentries, and the guard commander plucked up courage and went out with the new sentries and brought the old ones back with him. The dog followed them out, came back after them and lay down again in the same place.

After that not a man would go alone out of the guard-room, not all night. The rule was that at midnight the gate had to be locked and the keys carried to the Governor's room. Well, since not one of the soldiers would take them by himself, they drew lots and in the end the guard commander went along with the one that had to go.

After that, the dog used to come into the guard-room almost every night, and stretch itself out in the same place. Very often they didn't see it come, and there was never any question of hearing it, for it never made a sound. As long as they kept a steady watch-out for it to come, there was nothing to be seen: but sooner or later there'd be a moment when no one happened to be looking, and then they'd find it stood there in the doorway, staring round at them with eyes like glass when it catches the moon. There were no pupils in those eyes, or so I've been told: but just the same, they seemed to see all they wanted – and quite as much as the soldiers wanted, too. And it was no different when the dog went. The fire would fall in the grate, a bat would fly in or the wind would send a puff of smoke out into the room, and when they looked again it would be gone – sometimes at cock-crow, but sometimes long before that; just whenever it was called away, as they supposed, by – well, by whoever called it away, you know, sir.

It got so no one ever went about the castle alone at night. The sentries stayed in pairs, unless it was a night when they knew the dog wouldn't come. For it didn't always come. It didn't come at Christmas-time, nor at Easter-time neither, and now and then it didn't come for several days, for reasons they could only guess at; I mean, perhaps the one who sent it had – well, had work for it to do elsewhere, you know. No one ever spoke to the dog or went near it, and after a while the soldiers almost got used to it, for it seemed as though it would harm no one provided it was left alone, and there certainly wasn't any temptation for anyone to do otherwise – or so you'd have thought.

But then, one day, a new captain or lieutenant or some such arrived at the castle; sailed over from England, and brought quite a few of his own soldiers along with him. Several of them had already heard tell of the Moddey Dhoo and those who hadn't didn't take very long to learn about it, as you might suppose, and to make up their minds that the best thing for them would be just to fall in with its ways, like everyone else. But there was one fellow, a man they called Prating Jack – a real rip-roarer, as had been in and out of all manner of fights and skirmishes and was given to saying he wasn't afraid of man, beast or devil. It just so happened that for quite a while after this Prating Jack came to the castle the Moddey Dhoo didn't appear, so he had plenty of time to go boasting all over the place that if ever *he* met the dog it had better watch out, for he wasn't one to let any kind of dog interfere with anything that he might take a fancy to be doing.

Well, it seems there came a fine, clear night, with a full moon – very much like tonight, I dare say – and this Prating Jack, he was in the guard-room along with his mates, and they were playing cards. The keys hadn't been taken up to the Governor's room yet, for the gate had only just been shut, but two fellows – Manxmen – called John Corlett and Will of Ramsey, they'd been told to take them; and they were just off about it when Prating Jack, who'd been drink-ing, he upped and called them all manner of fools for believing in such nonsense as the Moddey Dhoo.

'Why,' says he, 'what a bunch of ignorant, silly, back-of-beyond Islanders you must be, to believe a lot of rubbish the like o' that! We've no Moddey Dhoos in London,' he says, 'and if we had we'd very soon put paid to them, I'll tell you. Dog or devil,' he says, 'it's all one to me; and if it can hear me I wonder it doesn't come and try

lifting its leg against the table, so's I can teach it some manners.' And then he threw his pewter-pot up in the air, but seems he was that fuddled that he stumbled catching it and knocked all the cards on the floor. They'd gone down after 'em and I suppose they were groping all around, when someone looked up and there was the Moddey Dhoo standing in the doorway. No sound, no shadow.

Then all the others stood away from Prating Jack and waited to see what he'd do. And Jack, he kind of waited too, for of course he'd never seen the Moddey Dhoo before and it wasn't quite what he'd been imagining, I dare say. After a few moments, though, he picked up the keys and walked across to the door.

'Out of the way!' he says to the dog. 'Look sharp!' And then they all got a shock, for the dog moved aside and let him go out of the room. He might have been gone as long as half a minute, perhaps, when it turned and went padding off, quite slow, the same way as he'd taken, with its head down and a kind of a curl to its lip – kind of a grin, like the jaws of a trap set open.

They felt sure, then, that something was going to happen, and they weren't wrong. I never heard how long he was gone, but however long it was, they just kept silence, listening. That must 'a been something to see, I should think, sir, shouldn't you – eight or nine of 'em, I dare say, all sitting there, waiting and listening, and just the moths and the moonlight coming in at the windows? In the end they heard pretty much what they were fearing – a terrible scream. But no one went out of that room, you can be sure. And then, presently, back comes Jack, pale as a sheet, staggering and shivering, and his face all twisted to one side and the mouth working for all the world as though he was chewing on a lump of dough. And they could get never a word out of him – not a word! He died two days later, and he was shivering all the time, right to the end.

The Moddey Dhoo? Well, they tell you different things, but some say it left the castle

alone after that, so that a great many people at the time wondered whether perhaps it mightn't have been after that Jack all along – knowing he was going to show up one day and not meaning to miss him, you know. But whatever the rights of that might be, it certainly hasn't left the Island. Oh no, it's been seen several times this century; and I'd rather you didn't smile, sir, really; not in my house, at all events. I don't want – well, never mind.

About fifty years ago there was a man saw it outside Ramsey, just by the turning up into Glen Auldyn. He told what he saw, and it was just the same as the dog at Peel Castle – all black and shaggy, and eyes like glowing coal, he said. He was terrified to pass it, but then the dog turned and left him, as though it had done whatever it came for. And so it had, for soon after that the man's poor father died. Then a few years after that, there was a doctor called out in the night to a farmer's wife having a baby, and just at that very same place *he* saw the dog, but it let him go by. It was still there when he came back two hours later, though I never heard of anyone dying that time. Well, he was a doctor, of course.

I wouldn't talk too much round here, sir, about what I've told you. Only, as I was saying, a lot of people take these things more seriously than you might suppose. Perhaps it's not so very surprising, really. The castle itself's closed at this time of night, but of course there's nothing to stop you and your lady from having a little stroll round under the walls, if you fancy it. No? Well, I don't blame you. I've enjoyed our little chat. As I was saying, we don't see many American visitors here. You'll have to excuse me now: here come two of my regulars, Mr Quayle and Mr Corlett. Think it'll blow before morning, Harry? Too strong for boats to go out? 'Dare say it might.

THE WOODPECKER

There she gows, look, that old Mrs Misery! See 'er dahn the bottom of 'er bit of garden, there – pokin' 'er old nose rahnd the corner of them sheets what she's 'angin' out? She reckons she c'n see into Mavis's kitchen winder from there, see? 'Avin' another good old sniff into what ain't none of 'er business. I was dahn the supermarket t' other day, 'avin' a bit of a rabbit to Sandra Wilson – you know, Sandra Green as was – on'y we was at school together, see – she's on the cheese cahnter now – all them foreign cheeses what rich people buys and they don't 'alf charge 'em, too, serve 'em right, I say, let 'em pay – and then I looks rahnd and there she is, old Misery, standin' just a little ways off, listenin' as bloomin' 'ard as ever she can, you'd wonder 'er flippin' ears don't make a draught, that you would. And when Mrs Tyler 'ad that trouble 'avin' the baby last April, what nobody expected

'er to, she's 'ad four, see, easy as roll-over, so the 'orspital says, 'Well, 'ave it at 'ome, dear, nice and comfy,' they says, an' then she was took that bad, and long before the amb'lance come old Misery, she'd got 'old of it all some'ow or other, an' up and dahn the street, in an' out of doors with it, like some bird of ill-omen what was in that there Count Drack'la film, I'd rather 'ave a nice love story, would'n you? You says it, she'll 'ear it! *An'* she'll tell it an' all. I declare on me owth I b'leeve if you was to whisper somethin' dahn the loo she'd 'ave it aht the sewer. Poke, poke, poke, mornin' to night and always other people's business. Proper ol' woodpecker, that's what she is.

Woodpecker? Well, you've 'eard that before, Jean, surely, 'aven't yer? That's what we always calls anyone goes on like that. It's a kids' story, aht of one of them old books. I c'n remember the teacher readin' it to us in class an' then after-wards we all 'ad to do a picture – *you* know – an' Sandra didn't do the woodpecker at all, she did one what was s'posed to be Dirk Bogarde on a bike, an' the teacher, she says 'What's this?' she says, an' there was me an' Sandra gigglin' fit to bust an' she picks it up – oh, yeah, I was tellin' yer abaht the woodpecker, wa'n't I?

Well, there was this old woman, see, only it was a long time ago, in olden days, sort of: an' she was always pokin' 'er long nose into other people's business, sniffin' abaht, eavesdroppin', inquisitive, pickin' up what didn't belong to 'er and makin' mischief with the neighbours an' that. Well, one day the neighbours decided at last as it 'ad all got so bad, see, they goes off to this magician bloke what lived t'other side the tahn – 'e bought foreign cheeses, I dare say – an' they says they'll give 'im ever such a lot of money if only 'e'll put a stop to 'er tricks for good 'n' all. So 'e says, 'All right', 'e says, 'I'll be rahnd to-morrer mornin' an' see if I can't just do a little bit for yer,' 'e says. So then they goes 'ome an' 'opes fer the best, see.

Well, so next day this old magician, 'e comes along, an' 'e's got a big parcel with 'im, see, just like Father Christmas dahn the bazaar. On'y 'e's disguised 'isself as a messenger bloke aht of one of the big stores. So then 'e waits till she comes aht of 'er 'ouse an' 'e follows her dahn the road, on'y 'er old man's gone off to see 'is sister for the day, see, an' now she's off dahn 'is allotment to get 'erself some vegetables. Well, while she's dahn there this old magician comes up, very civil-like, an' 'e touches 'is peaked cap an' all, kind o' respectful, an' 'e says, 'You Mrs So-and-So?' 'e says. So she says, 'Yes,' an' 'e says, 'Well, I got this 'ere big parcel,' 'e says, 'for Mr Morris, what 'as the next allotment to yours,' 'e says. 'They tells me dahn the shop 'e wants it delivered to 'is allotment shed. On'y 'e ain't 'ere. I was wonderin' if you could very kindly accept delivery,' 'e says, 'so's I c'n get done?'

'What's in it, then?' she asks 'im, very sharp.

'I dunno,' says the magician, 'but it says

"Open with care", so I dare say as it might be fragile goods, kind o' style. Still, you on'y got to lock it up in your shed,' 'e says, 'an' tell Mr Morris when you sees 'im – that's if you'll very kindly take the responsibility,' 'e says, 'an' sign for it. 'Course, if you feels you can't take it on –'

'Oh, no, no,' answers the nosey old woman, very quick. 'No, that'll be quite all right,' she says. 'I'll be seein' Mr Morris. I'll sign for it.' On'y she was dyin' to know what was inside the parcel, see?

'That's very kind of you,' says the magician. So then she signs 'is bit of paper what 'e's got all ready, an' off 'e goes. Or leastways, off 'e *seems* to go.

Well, soon as 'e'd gorn, the old woman takes the parcel inside of 'er own shed, an' she's sittin' lookin' at it an' thinkin' 'ow she can best open it an' see what's inside an' then put it all back again same as what it was before. It didn't look too bad a job, reelly, 'cause it was on'y just string an' brahn paper, an' she could feel this 'ere box what was underneaf. So after a bit she gets to pickin' away at the knots an' pullin' 'em loose, an' she's noticin' 'ow they're tied, so's she can do 'em all up again later on.

Well, she gets the knots undone an' pulls the paper orf, and then she decides she's goin' t'ave a go at the box, so she puts it up on a bench and tugs orf the lid. And blimey! she never 'ad such a shock in all 'er flippin' puff, 'cause what come aht was *insects* – fahsands of 'em, 'oppin' and flyin' an' scuttlin' all arahnd everywhere, some aht the winder and some under the bloomin' door an' some in 'er 'air an' all sorts. Cor, that was a right old lark, that was! On'y the magician, 'e'd filled it all up wiv insects on purpose, see, to catch 'er out in 'er nasty old ways. You're gownter say nothin' s' very magic about that, neether, but that was on'y just the beginnin', like, of all what 'e 'ad in mind. She was carryin' on somethin' dreadful, flappin' abaht with 'er 'ands an' pullin' 'em out of 'er 'air, an' the paper an' string all trampled under 'er feet an' I don't know what-all. An' then she 'ears someone comin', an' she squeals aht

''Elp! 'Elp!' On'y when she gets the door open, first thing she sees is the magician, an' this time 'e was dressed up like 'isself.

'What you done?' 'e says to 'er, very stern. 'You bin an' opened that there parcel what you'd got no business to open,' 'e says. 'You'd better just catch all them insects and put 'em all back again where they comes from,' 'e says, 'else you're goin' to find yourself in very bad bother indeed.'

Well, o' course, she could no more catch all them insects than what an 'orse can toast crumpets. On'y she was afraid of the magician and ashamed of being fahnd aht doin' what she didn' oughter, see, so she went pickin' all rahnd, an' she catches a few of 'em and then she gets madder and madder, till at last she 'as to give it up as a bad job.

'I reckon I'd better give you a bit of 'elp,' says the magician. 'You don't seem just exactly equipped for that there job what you got to do,' 'e says. An' then 'e takes out 'is big magic wand. 'Turn into a woodpecker!' 'e shouts, wivin' it all rahnd 'er 'ead. 'Gow on, turn into a bloomin' woodpecker!'

An' that's what she done. She turned into a woodpecker good an' proper, an' 'er long nose, what she was always pokin' into other people's business – that got turned into a long beak; on'y she kept 'er old green coat an 'er red 'at what she'd got on. And ever since that day she goes flyin' arahnd, pokin' into trees and posts and old fences, and anywhere where she reckons she's got a chance to catch some more of them insects what she let aht the box. And if ever she gets done, that there old magician'll let 'er turn back into an old woman again.

I wish 'e would, any road. Then it might be that old Mrs Misery's turn to 'ave a go at bein' a woodpecker fer a bit. Do 'er good, that would. Cor blimey, just look at 'er now, turnin' them old newspapers over on top o' the dustbins! I s'pose she reckons someone might 'ave chucked aht some 'ighly private correspondence what she can 'ave a go at. Bloomin' Russian spy! 'Baht 'er mark that'd be, an' all.

CRAB

It *has* been rather a long journey, hasn't it? But you've both been very good. In fact, I'm proud of you. You're getting so grown-up now, it won't be long before you're driving the car and I'm riding in the back. No, of course I know you won't *both* be driving the car at the same time, Ros., you ass. One will be driving and the other will be telling me a story – that'll be the way of it. Every now and then the senile Dad will be prodded to make sure he hasn't gone to sleep – what's that? No, don't *you* go to sleep before we arrive – not if you can help it. I'd like you to be able to make some sort of sense to Grannie when we get there. She's sure to be looking forward to your arrival very much, especially as it's six months since she last saw you. You can go straight off to bed as soon as you've had supper, and go on sleeping as long as you like in the morning.

A story now – to stop you going to sleep? All right, I'll have a shot. Actually, it's not very much further, now, so I'll try to think of a not-too-long one that'll just about fit in. Let's see – d'you know the one about Crab and the king's ring? All right, then, here we go. Julie, you can be Lord High headlight dipper. That's the lever – this one, here, O.K.? Yes, dip for cyclists too, if there are any.

Once upon a time there was a king who had the bad luck to lose a precious ring. He was very

much upset about it, partly because it was extremely valuable, but mainly because his wife, the queen, had given it to him on the day when they'd both been crowned. All the palace servants were ordered to hunt high and low, but nothing at all came of that; and this wasn't surprising, as you'll see for yourselves in a minute or two. Everyone who went out of the palace was searched by the royal guards, for the king thought, 'Well, if it's been stolen, at least I'll do my best to stop it being taken off the premises. If whoever's taken it only gets frightened enough, who knows? He might even put it back.'

However, the ring still didn't turn up, and the poor old king decided that he'd have to try something else. So he caused it to be proclaimed throughout the land that he'd give a large reward to any wizard, magician, soothsayer or astrologer who would come to the palace, get down to work and find out where the ring might be.

For several days no one turned up for the job. The truth was, nobody fancied it. The king was known to be rather a crusty old so-and-so, given to impatience and blowing his top, but apart from that, there was nobody who really felt that there was much chance of being able to find such a small thing as a ring, either with magic or without it. After a week the king doubled the size of the reward, and hoped that might produce a few applicants.

Now far inland, at the other end of the kingdom, there lived a crafty old peasant by the name of Crab. Crab had pulled off a number of clever deals and tricks in his time and he and his sharp old wife were known to have quite a nice little bit salted away against their old age. And one night, down at the pub, someone said to Crab, 'Why don't *you* have a bash at finding the ring, Crab? I bet you could, if you really put your mind to it.'

Well, at the time Crab just told the man not to be silly, but later that night, when he got home, he fell to thinking what a terrific triumph it would be for him all round the neighbourhood if only he could manage to find the ring by some means or another, and how it would put him and his wife in Easy Street for the rest of their lives. So he tried the idea on his wife; and she said, 'Well, Crab,' says she, 'you always had the cheek of the devil, and you could always talk your way in and out of anything. You might as well have a try, and if I know you I dare say something will come of it.'

So the long and short of it was that the next day Mr Crab dressed himself up as best he could to look like a learned magician, in a tall hat and a long, black cloak with stars stuck all over it, and off he goes, together with his wife, to the palace, giving his name as The Great Dr Vendalon. The king, who was just about desperate by this time, received them courteously, said Crab could certainly have a go at finding the ring and asked him what he was going to need to pursue his search.

Now the truth was that Crab hadn't as yet got the faintest idea how he was going to go about the job. It was all just a trick for him and his wife to get three good, free meals a day for as long as they could keep it up. So he explained to the king that he was a very scholarly and learned astrologer and that he meant to find out where the ring had got to by means of a painstaking programme of astrological studies, conducted in private.

'It may take some little time, your Majesty,' says he, 'because I've got to cover all the possibilities. I need a nice, quiet room and some pens, ink and large sheets of paper. I shall be honoured to report my progress to you as soon as possible.'

So Crab was given a nice, comfortable turret room high up in the palace, and all the paper he asked for. And there he sat all day, by a roaring fire, while the wind blew and the snow fell outside, eating the excellent meals that were brought up to him and drawing marvellous circles and cabalistic signs and stars and anything else he could think of all over the paper. But of course there was still no ring.

Now one cold winter's evening, after this had been going on for about three weeks, Crab's dinner was brought up by a different servant from the one he'd had before, and this servant turned out to be a cheeky, bumptious sort of fellow. He hung about the room chatting, and after a time he began to tease Crab and as good as told him he was nothing but a cheat and an impostor.

'How much longer d'you reckon you're going to be able to keep it up, old fellow?' he asked, picking his teeth with a splinter of kindling wood and winking at Crab as he began clearing the table. 'Even that fool of a king's going to smell a rat soon, you know.'

'I'm not going to need much longer now, as a matter of fact,' replied Crab. 'Not more than a day or two. Just look here, at this zodiac chart – although you won't understand it. But I do. I know already where the ring is, and with a very little more study I shall find out who took it as well.'

As soon as he'd said this he saw, just for a second, a flicker of alarm cross the impudent servant's face. The next moment he'd concealed it, and began saying that the chart was all rubbish – which was true, of course. But that was enough and more than enough for Crab. He told the man to hurry up and be off with the dishes, because he wanted to get back to work; and on the way downstairs, to be so good as just to ask his wife

49

to step up and join him. When she came, he told her he'd got an idea, and they had a good, long talk about it.

The next evening, when the servant brought up the dinner, Crab told him at once not to bother with laying the table, but just to put the tray down, for he wanted his help with an experiment. He'd pinned up his big zodiac chart on the cupboard door, and beside it he'd fixed a large picture of the ring, which the king had had made to help him in his studies.

'Now,' said Crab, 'just put your right hand on that picture of the ring, please, and your left on the centre of the chart, will you?'

The servant hesitated, and immediately Crab asked him what he was afraid of. At that he did as Crab had said, and as soon as he touched the chart on the cupboard door, a strange, female voice inside said 'Kendawar mar toomi, kendawar mar toomi!'

'Mar *toomi*?' thundered Crab, with terrific conviction.

'Mar *toomi*!' answered the voice in the cupboard. 'Mar toomi, toomi, *toomi*!'

'Thank you,' said Crab to the servant, very civil. 'Excellent! That's all! You can go now.' And with that he turned his back and went into the bedroom.

Now Crab, as I've said, was a really crafty operator, and he'd already realized that if he were to accuse the man straight out, he'd just deny it, and then, as Crab had absolutely no evidence, he'd be no further on. He just had to try to frighten it out of the man. He went to bed, and left the servant to go and do the same.

The next morning the servant came in early and told Crab straight out that it was he who had stolen the ring: and then he begged him not to give him away, or he'd lose his life. He was only a poor man's son, he said, and he was afraid he'd yielded to opportunity and temptation.

'Fine!' said Crab. 'Well, I'm only a poor man's son too, so I might just go in for a bit of yielding to opportunity myself. If you don't want to find yourself on the gallows, you'd better bring me

twenty gold pieces by this evening. We're both smart, my boy, but I'm the smarter by a short head, you see.'

The servant protested that he couldn't lay his hands on half that amount.

'Oh, I think you can,' said Crab, 'if you try hard. It's a great mistake, you know, for one rogue to let himself get caught by another. I know your sort, because I used to be one. If you can come by the king's ring, you can come by twenty gold pieces all right by supper time. And mind you bring the ring too,' he added, as the servant went out.

Well, the servant managed it – just – as Crab had thought he would: and when they were together again that evening and Crab had pocketed the gold, he said, 'Now, here's what you're to do. You just take the ring and feed it to that turkey down there in the yard, mixed up with a good handful of corn. Make sure you get the right one, too: that one with the long beak, see the one I mean?'

The servant went downstairs and Crab watched out of the window while he fed the ring to the turkey. As soon as he was sure the job had been done good and proper, he went off to the Lord Chamberlain and asked for an audience of the king. When he was conducted into the throne room, he said, 'Your Majesty, I'm delighted to be able to tell you that my long, hard studies have at last borne fruit. I can now tell you how to recover your ring. It's safe and sound, for my magic arts have enabled me to discover that it fell from a window and was swallowed by the biggest turkey in the poultry-yard. And that's where it is now.'

When the excited king had got his ring back, he was absolutely delighted, and ordered the court treasurer to present old Crab, the demon astrologer, with a large reward: and then he told him that before he went home, he and his wife must be his guests at a splendid dinner the following night.

Now the dishonest servant was determined to get even with Crab somehow or other, if he could, and he thought up a plan to make him look an absolute fool and disgrace him. One of the servant's tasks was to hold the king's horse when he returned from hunting, and the afternoon before the dinner, just as the king was dismounting, he said, 'May it please your Majesty, that Dr Vendalon who calls himself a great astrologer is nothing but an ignorant peasant. Why, he pretends to be a wise man, and widely travelled, and yet he's never even seen the sea. If you don't believe me, test him tonight when you talk to him at dinner. He won't even be able to name a single fish.'

That night, when they were all seated at dinner, the first course to be brought in was a splendid dish of crabs; and as soon as they were served, and one had been placed before the famous astrologer, the king said, 'Since you're such a widely-travelled man, Dr Vendalon, no doubt you can tell me the name of that creature you're just going to eat.'

There was a horrible pause as the poor astrologer bent over his plate. Everyone waited. Then he was heard to mutter, 'Oh, Crab, Crab, now you're in a real mess!'

'Ha! ha!' roared the king. 'Well done! So much for that stupid servant of mine! I'll sack him tomorrow! Have another glass of wine!'

So Mr Crab and his wife rode home in great style in a coach-and-pair, and lived happily ever after.

My goodness, I timed that well, didn't I? There's Grannie's house and I can see her moving about in the kitchen, can't you? That lighted window at the end, see? Ros.? Ros.? Oh, no! She's sound asleep!

THE CRIMSON PARROT

Private K'bui, the barrel of thy rifle is like an Arab's armpit! Come here and look down it. Dost thou think that when the white officer comes round and turns out the guard, he will not inspect arms? Since it is Capitan Asherburner, he will certainly do so, for he is one to find dust behind the door when it has been swept there out of the way. Then thou wilt be in trouble, and dost thou think I will let thee drag me there after thee, like an old woman with a billy-goat on a cord? Private M'Longa, thy cap-badge looks as though it were made of old cheese! Private Nyere, I would say that thou hadst fished up that belt from the bed of the river, if there were any rivers in this miserable, treeless country of Arab thieves. May the police dogs catch them and tear them all to pieces for sons and grandsons of slave-traders!

I heard the Capitan say to Sergeant Kwamba that when the war ends and Hittiler is dead, there will be a great parade in Engeland before Kingi Georgie, and that all parts of the army, white and black and Indian, will send their best men, who will salute Kingi Georgie and he will salute them, together with his queen and the beautiful young princesses. Dost thou think *thou* wilt be there, Private M'Longa, with that cap-badge of thine stuck upside-down on thy backside? And thou needst not laugh, Private Nandasi. Thou art no smarter. What have I done to be given this pile of elephant-droppings in place of soldiers, and the Capitan coming round before the moon sets? He will be coming from the camp, between the two petrol-stacks by the railway-siding, so we shall hear Private Keefa challenge him. That will give us enough warning to be ready to turn out.

Now, who has a cigarette for his guard commander? Oho, Private N'fwano, white man's cigarettes, eh, with the bearded sailor on the packet? I will not ask thee where they came from. There have been none in the N.A.A.F.I. these ten days past, that I know. Well, a good thief is a good soldier. This is better than the issue 'V' cigarettes, which are beyond doubt made by Arab thieves from the dung of camels.

Now, gather round the stove here. Private K'bui, make it up, and fetch the polish, the oil and the cleaning-rags. This guard was not inspected when it mounted, save by Sergeant

Kwamba, who knows how to inspect nothing but beer-pots and other men's wives. Therefore it is all the more likely that Capitan Asherburner will inspect it. I am not going to lose a stripe on your accounts. Everything will be cleaned – boots, belts, cap-badges, rifles. And while they are being cleaned, the corporal of the guard, who is as a mother to his lads, will pass the time by telling a tale.

Well, I know many tales, but this is one which none of you ignorant askaris from the bush will have heard, for it is a cunning tale, one told to me by a girl in Nairobi with whom I lived on that last leave before we sailed on the great ship to Port a Saida. Do you remember the shops in Nairobi, where the merchants sell toys and carved animals made of ivory? I saw an ivory goddess who stood upon a pedestal of carved spheres, one within another and yet another within that, all free and able to turn. Even so is this tale of mine.

Long ago, there lived in Mahenge a young African of boldness and resolution, a fine young fellow altogether, but desperately poor, for his father and mother had died of a pestilence when he was a child, and he had grown up in the house of his uncle, who gave him little and helped him not at all. One day, soon after he was full-grown, he thought in his heart, 'If I stay here in Mahenge I have no more chance of wealth or a good marriage than a wildebeeste among lions. I will look elsewhere.' So the next day, while his uncle lay drunk, he stole some of his money and set out to seek his fortune.

Spit on the boot, K'bui! How do you expect it to dazzle the eyes of Capitan Asherburner? It must shine like a girl's shoulders oiled for a dance. M'Beya – for that was the young man's name – travelled for many days by paths he did not know and through villages that knew not him: he crossed rivers and spoke with many men, and always there was less of his uncle's money. It seemed he could no more make his fortune than a louse can bake chapatis. He crossed the Great Ruaha and the Rufiji and came to Dar es Salaam,

and there he spent more money, and came near to losing his life among back-street thieves even more worthless than Sergeant Kwamba. And still he travelled on, through unknown kingdoms and strange, mountainous lands of the north, for he was afraid to remain in one place, lest by some chance his uncle should learn where he was.

Now one evening M'Beya was sitting, aimless and disconsolate, on a pile of stones between two shops in the bazaar of a remote city, with little in his purse and less in his belly. And as he was wondering where he might spend the night, a man came towards him carrying a crimson parrot in a cage. The parrot's feathers caught the sun and glowed like the tail-lights of the company truck, and M'Beya stared, for he had never before seen such a bird. Then, as the man with the cage drew near, he unexpectedly turned aside and sat down beside M'Beya on the pile of stones.

'Saideh, effendi,' said M'Beya. 'How goes it with thee?'

'Why, well enough, thanks be to God,' answered the man, 'but I'm tired out with making money and that's the truth of it. I've been selling birds all day and made a deal more than they cost me, but now I'd be glad to get off home to my supper, if only I could sell this one and get finished.'

'Why dost thou not take it home with thee?' asked M'Beya. 'It won't melt in the night and doubtless thou couldst sell it tomorrow.'

'All very well,' answered the man, 'but the trouble is, this one's a rare fine talker and he'll be talking all night, whether I cover his cage or not. I've had him two nights already and my wife's told me she won't stand for a third. Yesterday morning I sold him to a rich merchant, but that evening he found me out in the bazaar and said that if I would not take him back he would order his servants to beat me. I'd told him the parrot talked, but he said it talked more than he'd bargained for. So here am I, still carrying it, and I suppose I'll have to wring its neck and lose my profit for the sake of a quiet night.'

'Nay, that would be a pity,' said M'Beya. 'Such a fine bird. But thou sayest it talks? How can that be?' For as I have said, he had never seen a parrot before, let alone heard one talk.

At this moment the parrot cocked its head, looked at him, and said, 'Greetings, lord! I can make thy fortune.'

M'Beya was so much startled that he leapt to his feet and almost ran away, for to him this seemed like witchcraft. But the bird-seller, laughing, called him back, and persuaded him that he was in no danger and the parrot's talking was no trick. So M'Beya sat down again on the stones while the parrot talked, and thought that it was the greatest wonder he had ever seen and heard in his life.

At last he said to the bird-seller, 'Thou seest that I am no rich man, but only an unlucky one, yet I myself will buy thy parrot, if the price is not more than I possess.' For it seemed to him now that this bird was a marvel for which he would be content to go hungry and shelterless.

M'Beya gave all the money he had left for the crimson parrot and the man wished him good fortune and went on his way. It grew dark and M'Beya began walking towards the outskirts of the city, for if he had to spend the night in the open, he meant at least to find some solitary refuge where he could hope to be safe from cut-throats. While he was going down a dark alley near the river – and turning round continually for fear of finding a knife in his back – the parrot said, 'Why remain poor, master, when thou couldst be rich?'

M'Beya almost dropped the cage; but then, recovering himself, he set it on the ground and asked, 'How dost thou imagine that I can become rich?'

'Put thine ear close,' replied the parrot, 'that none else may hear.' M'Beya did so, and it went on, 'This is the street of the jewel merchants. Dost thou see the lamplight at yonder upper window? There, we may be certain, sits some skinflint old merchant counting his money at the end of the day. Let me out of the cage, and then

go and knock at his door. Tell the servant that thou hast a message for his master's ear alone. The merchant will come down to thee, rather than let thee go up to the room where his gold lies spread on the table. Tell him what thou wilt, so thou givest me time to fly in at the window and out again with a piece of gold.'

'But surely he will lock it away before he comes down?' said M'Beya.

'Not he,' replied the parrot. 'Is it not safe in an upper room, with none in the house but himself and his servants?'

M'Beya released the parrot and then, having found the right door in the darkness, knocked and told the servant that he desired to speak with his master. When the old Arab merchant came down, he was ready enough with a tale of being one of the company of an Indian sea-captain, come from Malabar to trade silks and spices for rubies. When he had talked for as long as he could, and arranged for his captain to call the next day, he bowed low and departed; and as soon as the door was closed, found the parrot on his shoulder even before his eyes had grown once more accustomed to the dark.

'No matter the cage,' said the parrot. 'I will not leave thee. Here are three gold pieces. If thou hadst talked longer they would have been four. Let us go to a good inn and sleep in comfort.'

The following day, with the crimson parrot on his shoulder, M'Beya went down to the harbour, where he bought a passage on a ship bound for another city. She set sail at noon, and as soon as they were well under way, M'Beya seated himself under an awning in the bows to enjoy the cool breeze, while the parrot perched aloft in the rigging, among the gulls and other sea-birds which always frequent a ship at sea.

Towards evening, when M'Beya, rocked by the gentle movement of the ship, had fallen asleep, he was wakened by the parrot pulling at his ear.

'Listen, master,' said the parrot, 'we are in great danger. Before noon tomorrow there will be a storm.'

'How canst thou suppose that?' replied M'Beya. 'Look, the sea is calm as a bowl of milk.'

'The gulls told me,' said the parrot. 'Every one of them is agreed that a storm is coming down on us from the north. We should make for the nearest port at once. Warn the captain, master.'

M'Beya did his best to tell the captain of their danger, but both captain and sailors laughed at him and, when he persisted, grew angry, telling him – which was true – that he knew nothing of the sea or of ships; and that he had better leave such matters to those who understood them. By dawn next morning, however, the sky had grown dark and the wind had risen. Within the hour a heavy squall broke over the ship. The sailors now became convinced that M'Beya must be a great wizard, who could foresee the future and control the weather, and they crowded round, entreating him to save their lives. M'Beya, who was inwardly as terrified as they, contrived to appear undisturbed and said that, although the spirits of the storm had been angered by their mockery and contemptuous treatment of him yesterday, he would neverthe- less do what he could: whereupon the captain gave him five gold pieces, explaining that it was all he had with him, but that he would give him more if only they could come safe to land.

For two days the ship was driven far across the ocean, into waters unknown to the captain and crew, but then the storm at last abated. Next morning they sighted land and soon after entered the harbour of a strange and wealthy city. The inhabitants, seeing M'Beya come ashore amidst the blessings and admiration of the ship's crew and his fellow-passengers, concluded that he must be some great personage; and that evening, while he was eating dinner at the city's best inn, he received a visit from the vizier of the Sultan. After much flattery and courtier's talk, the vizier told M'Beya that his fame as a prophet and magician had reached the ears of the Sultan, who desired him to come to the court and use his powers to save his eldest daughter.

'What ails her?' asked M'Beya. 'Is it a sickness?'

'It is no sickness,' replied the vizier. 'Indeed, the princess is the fairest maiden in the land and just of an age to marry. Several fine young princes and noblemen have already asked her hand in marriage and no less than six in all have been wedded to her. But she is in the power of an evil sorcerer, one in league with the spirits of darkness. He comes by night and none can ward him off, for he flies through the air and is guarded by demons. To the princess herself he does nothing, yet no man who becomes her husband will he suffer to live. Thus through his evil jealousy these six fine young men have all been strangled.'

'By what means did he overcome them?' asked M'Beya.

'Any man,' replied the vizier, 'who would set the princess free from his power must bind himself to contest with him in three trials. If it were possible to defeat him in each of the three, he would – so he has himself given out – be overthrown and forced into imprisonment by those very powers of darkness who now serve him. But as yet no man has been able to succeed in even one of the trials. Indeed, to do so would be impossible to any but a magician as powerful as himself. This is why the Sultan entreats thy help. If thou art indeed a wizard, it may be that thou canst defeat this sorcerer and free the princess from his power. He who could do so – if any such there were – would become rich and full of honour, and reign as successor to the Sultan himself.'

'What are the trials?' asked M'Beya.

'The first,' answered the vizier, 'is to pass bodily through a narrow cleft in the palace ramparts, no wider than a man's hand. The second is to climb the sheer wall of the palace to the highest minaret above its roof. These feats are sufficiently impossible, yet the third is enough to make them appear simple. The sor- cerer, who dwells upon the inaccessible summit of a mountain overlooking the city, has said that he who would overthrow him must reach that summit from the palace faster than he can get there himself. Yet since he flies through the air, none can hope to succeed. But have no fear, young man,' added the old vizier, seeing M'Beya's look of dismay. 'The Sultan is a just and kindly ruler, and has instructed me to assure thee that he will not force thee or any other man to attempt these impossible feats. The reason I am here, as I have said, is that we heard that thou possessest magic powers; and on this account the Sultan, in his sorrow and great need, dared to hope that perhaps thou wouldst be willing to help us. But I see that thou hast no mind to throw thy life away; nor can I blame thee. I will inform the Sultan of thy regret that the matter is beyond thee.'

'But why did the six young men who died attempt these impossible contests?' asked M'Beya.

'The princess is so beautiful,' replied the vizier, 'that all who see her fall in love with her on the instant. Each of the young men felt himself ready to attempt anything in order to be her husband.'

At this moment the inn-keeper, entering the room, told the vizier that a petitioner was waiting outside to see him. While the vizier was gone the parrot said to M'Beya, 'Master, tell the Sultan that thou wilt defeat this sorcerer. Only put a bold face on the matter and I will contrive all.'

'But how can I succeed in these feats?' asked M'Beya. 'I shall but die like the rest.'

'Trust me,' answered the parrot. 'I shall find the way.'

M'Beya was by no means persuaded, but when the vizier returned he told him that at any rate he would, as a matter of courtesy, visit the palace next day and pay his respects to the Sultan,

though he could not promise to undertake the contest with the sorcerer. The truth was that he felt a great desire to see the beautiful princess: and besides, he had never in his life been inside a Sultan's court.

The following morning, having spent all his remaining money on the best clothes he could buy, he made his way to the palace with the crimson parrot perched on his arm. The old Sultan received him courteously and asked him many questions about his magical knowledge and the dangerous voyage during which he had stilled the tempest; for the tale, like most sailors' tales, had lost nothing in its telling about the city.

While they were thus talking together, the Sultan's daughter entered the presence chamber. The moment M'Beya saw her, he became so enraptured that he was ready at all hazards to win her for his bride or die in the attempt, for without her, he felt, life would no longer be worth living. At the first opportunity he begged her father to agree that they should be married that very day, and promised that he would undertake the deadly combat with the sorcerer. The old Sultan, thanking him gravely, replied that since he himself wished it to be so, he was ready to do anything that might help him in his desperate venture.

M'Beya asked to be permitted to reflect for a time in solitude, and as soon as he was alone asked the parrot what was to be done. 'For,' said he, 'my life is in thy keeping. Without thee I can do nothing, yet if we fail I shall not blame thee, for now that I have seen her I would rather die than live without the princess.'

'Tell the Sultan,' answered the parrot, 'that thou dost wish to see the narrow cleft upon the ramparts through which the sorcerer will pass tonight. Also, ask for a bag of shelled almonds and as thou art walking upon the ramparts, strew them all along between the cleft and the princess's bedchamber.'

M'Beya, having made these requests, was conducted along the ramparts to the cleft, no wider than a man's hand, within which was a stone cell with a locked and bolted door. When he realized the total impossibility of entering the cell through this cleft, his heart fell, for he had hoped that he might have been able to overcome the sorcerer by some trick. Nevertheless, he did as the parrot had advised and while returning strewed the nuts along the rampart walk.

That evening the marriage ceremonies were performed and as darkness fell and then grew deep – for it was a moonless night – M'Beya and the beautiful princess went together to her apartments within the upper rampart wall. Here the parrot instructed M'Beya to conceal himself and, when the sorcerer came, to remain hidden and on no account to speak a word.

At midnight the terrible sorcerer appeared upon the ramparts, having soared down from his dwelling upon the mountain-top above the city. Putting to flight the guards and flinging open the door of the bridal chamber, he assailed the bridegroom with dire threats, telling him that if he did not at once forsake his bride and flee the country for ever, he must enter upon a contest the outcome of which could only be his certain death. Then, from the darkness, the parrot answered, insulting the sorcerer and enraging him with taunts and jeers, so that he rushed into the room to come to grips with the young man who dared thus to defy him. The parrot, flying silently out of the door, cried to him from outside to make haste to the cell within the narrow cleft. Finding its way in the darkness by the smell of the cloven almonds, it flew to the cleft, entered the cell and concealed itself in a crevice; and when the sorcerer reached the place, again taunted him, saying that a greater magician was now here to overthrow him – one that could become invisible at will. At this the sorcerer departed in great anger, promising to return the following night and slay his enemy.

Next day the parrot told M'Beya to request of the Sultan that at nightfall a brazier of charcoal and a bundle of brushwood should be carried up to the highest minaret above the palace roof, together with a table, a longsword, a pitchfork and the hearts and livers of two or three bullocks. At midnight the evil sorcerer again appeared, and once more the parrot defied him, finally calling out that if he really supposed that he could kill him, he had better make haste to the minaret above the palace roof, whither he himself was about to climb. When the sorcerer reached the minaret he looked about him in the light of the brazier, but could see no one.

'If thou art here, young man,' he shouted, 'reveal thyself!'

'I have been here some time,' replied the parrot, concealed among the brushwood, 'but I see no need to reveal myself to a fool like thee. Kindly go away and leave me in peace. I am about to cook for supper the hearts and livers of some sorcerers I killed this afternoon. There is my cutlery, propped up against the table. Perhaps thou wilt kindly sharpen the knife for me, since it looks a trifle blunt.'

At this the sorcerer once more made off to the mountain, while the parrot returned to M'Beya and the princess. M'Beya was now elated and full of hope, but the parrot said to him, 'Master, the most severe trial is still to come and in this thou must play thy part, for I cannot succeed alone. Go to the Sultan and ask him to command his soldiers to bring a fisherman's net, as strong as may be found, and to spread it open, fastened to stout poles thrust into the crevices of the stone-work below the rampart walls. Tonight, when the sorcerer comes, reveal thyself openly and say that thou art ready to fly to the mountaintop. Only contrive to delay the business for as long as thou canst, for I shall need time if all is to go well.'

'Will this be sufficient?' asked M'Beya.

'Three things more,' replied the parrot. 'Have ready on the ramparts a bag of offal and sheep's guts and a cut of tender meat, well-cooked with spices. Send some soldiers to the foot of the mountain to light a fire and keep it burning throughout the night. And let me have a seal, cut in the likeness of the Sultan's own.'

M'Beya caused all to be done as the parrot had told him and that night again awaited the coming of the sorcerer, knowing that this time he would be employing all his evil powers to take from him both his beautiful bride and his life. When the sorcerer appeared, M'Beya told him that now, since he was about to defeat and destroy him, he would reveal himself openly. Then he pretended to have second thoughts and to feel hesitation, and began asking the sorcerer whether they might not come to terms, offering him gold and jewels if he would depart and leave him in peace. Meanwhile the parrot slipped out of the room and, catching up in its claws the piece of roasted meat and the bag of offal, began its flight to the summit of the mountain.

At length the sorcerer, perceiving M'Beya's apparent reluctance and thus regaining the courage he had lost the night before, cried out that his patience was exhausted and that M'Beya must now either face him in the third and last contest or die forthwith. He further demanded that this time M'Beya should not make himself invisible, but stand forth upon the ramparts where he could be seen. Thereupon M'Beya, crying out 'I will be on the mountain-top before thee!', walked boldly to the edge of the wall and cast himself forth into the dark, falling silently and unharmed into the net spread below.

Soon afterwards the parrot, flying above the city and the fields beyond, reached the sorcerer's dwelling on the mountain-top. Here the sorcerer had left as guardian his attendant demon, a terrible creature in the form of a great hound with fangs as sharp as razors. It was his custom, when he put the place in the beast's care, to leave it unfed until he returned, so that it should be the more alert and fierce. As the parrot approached the hound sprang forward, growling and threatening to devour it if it should alight.

'Why, as to that,' said the parrot, 'make thyself easy, for I have brought thee a good supper. Catch it!' And thereupon it threw down the savoury meat, which the hound devoured in one gulp.

'How was that?' inquired the parrot.

'Good! Good, but little enough!' answered the

hound. 'Not enough for a beast like me, that eats two oxen a day!'

'That is easily put right,' replied the parrot. 'Dost thou see yonder fire burning at the foot of the mountain? That is my camp, where the Sultan's soldiers are roasting no less than *five* oxen. Hasten there, and tell them I sent thee.'

'This is some trick,' said the demon. 'I will not go.'

'Indeed it is not,' replied the parrot, taking good care to keep at a safe distance. 'I am of the Sultan's household and carry his seal to prove it.'

With this the parrot dropped the imitation seal on the ground before the demon who, seeing the Sultan's emblem, required no more persuasion and went baying off towards the fire at the foot of the mountain, leaving the parrot alone to strew the offal upon the ground.

Soon after, there was heard a rushing wind and the sorcerer appeared. No sooner had he alighted than the parrot cried out, 'Thou dawdling ass, I have already awaited thee too long, and now I have once more made myself invisible,

in order that I may kill thee the more swiftly and easily. As for that foolish demon in whom thou didst trust to guard thy dwelling, I have sliced him up and strewn his guts upon the ground. See where they lie!'

At this the sorcerer, despairing of all his powers against such an adversary, made off across the desert howling with fear, while the parrot flew back to M'Beya and the princess. The good old Sultan, when told of the sorcerer's defeat, at once declared a week's holiday and rejoicing for all the kingdom, at the end of which he publicly declared M'Beya his heir and successor. The parrot was given a cage of gold and a jewelled chain –

Hark! Private K'bui, stop brushing that belt and be silent! Ay, that is Private Keefa challenging Capitan Asherburner, who will therefore be here directly to turn out the guard. Nyere, the magazine is out of thy rifle! N'fwano, thy belt is on upside-down! Remember, we turn out at the slope, and God help any man who strikes his barrel against the top of the door!

THE LANGUAGE OF
ANIMALS

Yes, of course it will be a boy, my darling – the finest ever born from Charva to Brel. You wait and see – and you won't have to wait long, either. You know what my old grandmother used to say? 'A good tinder catches the first spark.' How many boys do you want, farmer – my farmer, my ploughman? Six, seven? Big, strong boys – ah, and then you'll spend all day sitting idle in the porch, under the honeysuckle; yes, sit in the sunshine and drink your beer while they do the work. All you'll be ploughing then'll be the midnight furrow, no danger.

Now do you know you've got a better bargain than Airsovitz? Oh, ho! Never looked at Airsovitz, eh, nor her blue ribbons that match her eyes? I saw you, yes, when she was sitting under the chestnut trees, down by the mill. Ah, it makes me laugh *now*. Don't you think I can afford to laugh, and me in the arms of the finest lad in all the Kestcheva?

Let the lamp burn, my darling – why go to sleep yet? Don't you like looking at me? There's oil enough in the house, yes, and wine and cheese and bacon and apples and flour for that matter, and a lot more. I'll cook it and you eat it. The cooking? You dare to tell me it was all along of my cooking, and me lying stretched out here like a beach after a spring tide? Come September, when I'm like the water-butt in the yard, you tell my mother it was all along of the cooking. Don't forget!

Oh, look, there's a mouse, see – there, in the moonlight by the door? No, of course I'm not afraid of them; that must be Airsovitz. Nor rats neither, as long as we've three good cats in the house. No, bide still, dear. Let it be, just for tonight. I'll soon clear the house of mice for you – that and a lot more. The room across the passage will make a fine nursery.

Ah, he heard me, the mouse! Did you hear what he said? What, you don't understand the language of animals, and you a farmer, and your father and grandfather before you? Well, you've a lot to learn then, my ploughman. We'll send you to school to old Thomas, to learn the talk of the beasts and how to be master in your own house. Else they'll all be laughing at you. Yes, they will. Don't you give me every last thing ever I could want for? That's no way to treat a wife, you know – 'makes them harder to manage than a mare that's been six weeks out to grass. Oh, you like me that way, do you?

You don't know the tale? You *don't?* I know something you don't, farmer? Well, then, you're not so old yet but you can listen to a bedtime story, my little lad. What? Littler than you were just now, anyway. And I need some practice. I'll be telling stories soon instead of listening to them. Put your arm under my head. That's right.

That's thick enough to keep out trouble, I reckon.

There was once a shepherd named Thomas, who'd served his master very well for a long time. He used to be out in all weathers – knife, tarbox and hurdles – and never lost a yow nor yet a lamb, even when the mist was down low as the fields. It was a solitary sort of a life he had, for he'd never married; but he didn't complain of that, nor yet of nothing else.

Thomas was an honest, decent, straightforward fellow, as everyone was agreed. They used to say he was one man who hadn't a notion how to begin to deceive another, and that he could no more lie than fly. Some of them even said he was a bit too kind and honest, and that was why he was still another man's shepherd instead of master of a nice bit of farmland of his own. There was one fellow said this straight out to him one day, but Thomas just laughed and said he wasn't bothered himself and why should anyone else be?

Now, one fine day in a dry October, Thomas was out on the hillside with his dogs, having a look round for any woolled sheep that might have got overlooked at clipping time, when all of a sudden he saw a patch of gorse and heather on fire a little way down below. It hadn't got too far at all, but there was no one else to be seen and the wind was taking it a bit, so Thomas left the dogs to look after the two or three sheep he'd picked up and ran down to beat it out.

When he got down to it he had more of a job than he'd bargained for, only the heather was dry and the fire was going a bit faster than he'd reckoned. Anyway, get it under he did in the end, and he'd just come to the last of the blaze, which was all in a kind of a ring round a patch of open grass, when he saw a snake darting this way and that in the middle, and no way out for it neither.

When the snake saw Thomas it called out, 'Save me, shepherd, save me! Else I'll be burned!'

'Be danged if I do!' says Thomas. 'Save a snake? Reckon I'm daft?' he says.

'You'll be well rewarded, I promise you,' says the snake. 'Save me, Thomas! You'd save a lamb, wouldn't you? It's a hard death in the fire.'

'Well, it is that,' says Thomas. 'All right, call me a fool, here goes.'

And with that he puts the point of his old crook right over the flames and down on the grass the other side, and that snake was up it faster than a gypsy grabs a pheasant. He was up Thomas's arm and round his neck snug as a hangman's halter, and Thomas reckoned there wasn't much difference neither, if the snake

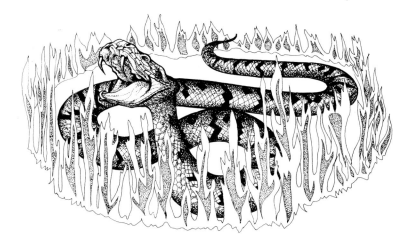

should take a fancy to make sure his teeth were still in working order after the fire. Just the feeling of the snake round his neck made the soles of his feet tingle.

'Steady, now, steady,' he said to the snake. 'One good turn deserves another, you know.'

'It does,' replied the snake. 'That's why I want you to carry me back to my father's palace. He's the king of all the snakes and he'll reward you well for saving my life. Will you take me?'

'I don't see that I've much choice, all things considered,' thought Thomas. 'What about my sheep?' he asked. 'Dogs won't bide forever without shepherd, you know.'

. 'They'll be safe enough, trust me,' says the snake.

So off they went, round the wood and up the rocks. And when they got to the top, there was a door in a big crag, all made of live snakes twined together, in and out. When they saw the snake round Thomas's neck, they opened up, all hissing and bowing their heads, and in he went, right into the heart of the hill.

'Now,' says the snake, 'in a moment we'll be in my father's hall. And he'll offer to give you whatever you like for saving my life – gold and silver; and rubies too, I wouldn't wonder. But don't you go accepting them. You ask him for the power to understand the language of animals. He'll try to put you off and dissuade you, but just you stick to it and I promise you won't regret taking my advice.'

Well, they came into the hall and sure enough there was the snake-king sitting there and enough snakes all around to frighten the life out of a parson and into his dog, as the saying goes. The king asked his son where he'd been and what he was doing all wrapped round the neck of a nasty, warm-blooded shepherd. But when the snake had told about the fire and Thomas's kindness, sure enough his father thanked Thomas very kindly and said there were few enough men these days, more was the pity, would do that much for a snake. And then he told him to name his reward.

'There's my treasure-house round the back,' says he. 'Perhaps you'd just like to take a look through it, Thomas, and pick out whatever you fancy.'

But Thomas, who trusted everyone and believed all he was told, did as his friend had advised and said that if it was all one to the king he'd like to be gifted with the power of understanding the language of animals.

'You're a great fool, Thomas,' says the king., 'You'd do better to choose something else, for just you mark my words; if I give you that power, the very minute you tell your secret to any other human being, you'll fall down dead as a rabbit in a harvest-field, and that's the plain truth.'

Well, Thomas answered up and said he was a solitary man both by nature and occupation and didn't do much in the way of talking as a rule; and then he said he thought it would come in very handy to pass the time on the hillside if he was able to understand his dogs and sheep – and the crows and linnets too, come to that. The king asked him again to change his mind, but he wouldn't, so then the king gave way and agreed to what he asked for. There was a kind of a ceremony went with it, and Thomas and the king blew breath into each other's mouths while they stood in a magic circle; and then the king himself conducted Thomas as far as the door and told him if he valued his life on no account to mention a word to anyone about the power he'd been given.

As Thomas was making his way back to his dogs and sheep, he found he could understand everything the birds were singing in the trees. And as he came up the hill he heard one of his dogs say, 'Look out, you fellows, here comes old Thomas back again,' and another replied, 'About time, too. Leaving us here to do all the work.'

Now later on that day Thomas was sitting under a bank, having a bite of bread and cheese, when he heard two old ravens croaking together in a thorn-tree. One said to the other,

'Remember those robbers I was telling you about? Over there, where that old black sheep's grazing, see – that's where they buried their treasure, and that's fifty years ago and more.'

'What became of it?' asks the other.

'Why, it's still down there,' answered the first raven. 'The robbers were all hanged next year and never told anyone where they'd put the treasure. My father and I were the only living creatures that saw them digging – ay, and we picked their bones on the gibbet not a twelve-month after.'

When he heard that, Thomas drove the sheep home to the farm and went and told his master that he knew where there was buried treasure on his land. And seeing as Thomas had never deceived him or anyone else in all his life, his master just takes a spade and goes along with him to the place. They had to dig down a fair old way, but in the end they came on the treasure sure enough, and plenty there was, too.

'Now look here, Thomas,' says his master, who was a decent, kindly sort of a man. 'How you came to know about this I don't know and I'm not asking; but you've served me honestly and well these twenty years and you came and told me about it when you might have kept it a matter between yourself and the moonlight. You're going to keep four-fifths of this and I'll just content myself with the rest, and no argument, now. And if I were you I'd buy myself a nice little farm and take on some young fellows to do the hard work. Then they can keep sheep in the rain and you can walk about the place and tell them what to do next.'

Thomas did as his master suggested and a bit more than that, for what with being both well-to-do and well-liked by everyone round about, it wasn't long before he'd got himself a handsome young wife, with blue ribbons – oh, yes, to be sure – and pink ribbons and three or four bonnets for going to church in. And since he soon got the reputation of being a very decent man to work for, he had all the hired help he needed.

His wife was a fine, smart girl, but didn't she

just know how to dance the I want polka? It was 'I want this' and 'I want that' from Monday to Saturday, and she never lifted a finger in the house, neither. There was a girl to do the cooking and another to sweep the floors and the missus's job was spending the money thank you very much and where's the rest? Nor she wasn't one to take No for an answer to anything. It's a wonder there was a stone left in the yard, what with her tongue going drip, drip, drip till it got through the other side of anything Thomas might have to say. And then after a bit she found her belly was bigger than before, and then it was 'I want' all the more, slap-slap-slap like a millwheel.

Now one day, just around Christmas-time and the fields colder than a good dog's nose, Thomas, like the decent fellow he was, had a mind to give a bit of a feast to all his men and maids, and he says to his bailiff, 'You can send the shepherds along as well. I'll watch the sheep myself while they just have a good blow-out for once. I know what it's like for a shepherd on his own this time of year; and as for me, it'll be like old times.'

Well, as Thomas was sitting out there in a wildish sort of a spot and the light going, what should he hear but five or six wolves a little way off in the wood. And as they got nearer, he realized that they were howling to his dogs.

'We're coming to get your sheep,' calls the pack leader. 'Don't resist us, and as soon as we've chased off that fool of a shepherd we'll let you have a share.'

Thomas waited to hear what his dogs would have to say to that, and he wasn't best pleased, to say the least of it, when two out of the three of them told the wolves they wouldn't so much as raise a hackle. But the third dog, old Captain, that he'd had by him all of ten years, barked out on his own that he'd be torn to bits before he'd let a parcel of dirty wolves come chewing up his master's sheep. All the same, the odds seemed a bit too long to Thomas. He just stayed long enough to blaze off with his old gun into the

trees and then he drove the whole flock down into the nearest barn as quick as he could.

Next day he was due to go to market with his wife, him on his old mare and her on her gelding – a nice, quiet thoroughbred she'd gone and bought for herself without telling Thomas what she had in mind. Thomas had never really cared for that gelding, although it was such a beauty, because he knew very well that the man who sold it to her would have taken a whole lot less for it – and so he would have done if Thomas had been given the chance to have a say in the matter.

The first thing he did when he got to market was sell the two dogs who'd let him down, and as they were young and strong and well-trained, he got a fair price for them, too, for of course he couldn't and didn't tell the reason why he was selling them. After that he did quite a bit more business here and there and I dare say he might have had a couple of drinks as well, for there were always plenty of people ready to stand him a drink, and he wasn't the sort not to buy them one in return.

He'd arranged to meet his wife at the market cross and when he got there he found she'd seemingly bought half the town. Her horse was all hung about with parcels and boxes and she was wearing a brand-new bonnet covered with – yes, with blue ribbons. Anyhow, they started off on the road, but before long the mare was out in front, even though Thomas had never touched her. He stopped for his wife to catch up, but 'twasn't long before the same thing happened again, and this time he could tell his old mare was very fidgety at being reined in.

As his wife came up, the mare said to the gelding, 'Can't you get a move on? Sooner we're home, you know, the sooner we'll get a feed and a rest.'

'All very well for you,' answers the gelding. 'You're only carrying the master, and his pockets are pretty well empty, if I'm any judge. And here's me carrying this girl with her great fat belly and a hundred and one parcels. She was hour and a half over dinner, I might tell you. Talk about eat for two –'

At this Thomas couldn't stop himself busting out laughing, and he sat on his old mare in the road and laughed till he cried.

'And what, pray, d'you think you're laughing at?' says his wife, very stiff.

'Oh, nothing, nothing,' answers Thomas. 'Nothing at all, my dear.'

'Nonsense!' says his wife, very sharp. 'I insist on your telling me, Thomas, what you were laughing at.'

'I assure you 'twas nothing at all, my dear,' says poor Thomas. 'I was just laughing, you know.' It sounded pretty thin, even to himself.

'If you reckon that I reckon that you go about the world laughing at nothing at all, then you must think I think you're going out of your mind,' says Mrs Thomas. 'Is that what you think I reckon you think I reckon, or is it not?'

'No, no, my dear,' says Thomas, 'only you see the trouble is if I tell you what I was laughing at, I shall die the next minute.'

'Laughing, I suppose,' snorted Mrs Thomas. 'Well, it's my belief you were laughing at me for some reason or other, and I'll get to the bottom of it, so help me Bob I will,' she says.

And she was on at him all the way home and she hardly gave him any sleep neither, going on and on. Poor Thomas thought up all sorts of things he might have been laughing at, but he was such a poor hand at that kind of game that she only got madder the more he went on. By next morning he was that put about he was just minded to make an end of it at any price. And the long and short of it was, off he went to the village carpenter and told him to bring a good, big coffin up to the house directly, and ask no questions neither.

When the coffin came, Thomas had it set up on trestles in the yard and then he lay down in it, and then he says to his wife, says he, 'Now I'll tell you what I was laughing at, and you'll be pretty near

as sorry as I am, for the moment I tell you, that'll be my lot – I shall die.'

'Fiddle-de-dee!' says she. 'I never heard –'

'It ain't fiddle-de-dee, neither,' says Thomas. 'This is the way of it, my dear. The fact is, I can understand the –'

Just at that moment, up comes poor, faithful old Captain, and he was fair howling his head off. Thomas felt sorry for him and he threw him a bit of bread as he had in his pocket, but Captain wouldn't touch it. He just left it lying in the dirt and after a moment the cock came across the yard and began pecking at it.

'Why, you deserve to have your neck wrung, that you do,' says old Captain to the cock. 'Here's the best master in the world lying in his coffin and just going to die, and you've still got stomach enough for pecking at bread! Be off before I kill you myself!'

'Pooh!' answers the cock. 'Good master he may be, but he's a blame fool for all that. Fancy letting a silly chit of a wife drive him out of his wits and into the next world, just like that! And he's only got *one*! Look at me! I've got twenty hens here and there's none of them dares try any nonsense with me! They'd better not!'

When Thomas heard that he burst out laughing again, and he jumps up out of the coffin and takes his wife by the two shoulders.

'Now, my dear,' says he, 'that's enough of that, d'ye understand? We'll have some peace and quiet round here in future, or you'll be making me laugh the other side of my face. So just watch out! And now we'll go indoors and have a drink together, nice and comfortable.'

And peace and quiet he had from then on, and no one ever had the secret from him, what's more. So you see, my dearest, there's a lot for you to learn yet, don't you think? You've still to find the right way to go about it – the right way to – oh, my love! Oh, wait! Wait! Ah, my darling, my love – ah! – ah! –

THE BLIND BOY
AND HIS DOG

Ah Fong! Ah Fong, you little mischief, come back here and out of the restaurant this minute! No, that is silly. If you hide under the table all that will happen is that I shall come and drag you out. It will be easier to do as I tell you – and more dignified. You are not too little to be learning to think of your dignity – especially here, in this land of foreign devils at the world's end. Ah, that's a good boy. Come and sit in the kitchen while I cook. No, I'm not angry. You can sit here by the fire and finish up this jar of lychees.

You thought it would be acceptable to play on the floor of the restaurant because no foreign devils have yet come to eat? Ah, but look outside – already it is dark and the restaurant is lit. We want the foreign devils who pass by to look through the big glass windows and think 'That appears to be a clean, tidy place, with coloured lanterns shining on the tablecloths. Let us go inside and buy a good dinner.' What will they think if they see a dirty little Chinese boy crawling round a floor littered with his toys? They will go three streets away, to Kuek Choon Chuan, and then we lose customers, and so there is less money. Your father works hard. Yu Shin works hard, and I too. One day there will be enough money, and we shall go home to Hong Kong and live in a fine house, with coolies to work for us; and you shall be a Chinese

gentleman and wear embroidered silk. But this can happen only if many foreign devils come to the restaurant and tell each other what a fine place it is.

What, you don't believe you'll wear embroidered silk in Hong Kong? Nay, but you will, my darling. Many stranger things have happened. We Chinese travel all over the world to make money, but we go home to China when we are rich. God sees all, and a good boy who learns to do as he is told and to work hard need never fear that life will pass him by. Lo-Sun was nothing but a blind beggar-boy, yet all came right for him in the end; and that was because he deserved it.

Who was Lo-Sun? Come over here, dear heart, and pass me the things I need from the table to finish this chop suey. A big pot, isn't it? It will all be gone before tomorrow. Give me the salt bottle – that's right. Now that plate of bamboo shoots and the wooden spoon. Good.

It was my grandfather who first told me the tale of Lo-Sun; and that was long ago, when I was no older than you are now. Grandfather lived in Kowloon, and my mother used to take me on the ferry-boat to visit him. One day I'll take you on that ferry-boat too. It's exciting in Kowloon at New Year, when the coloured dragons dance and the fireworks crackle up and down the streets.

Lo-Sun was a boy who was born blind – yes, in China, long ago. As soon as he was old enough to go about the place by himself, his mother gave him a dog which was trained to guide him and keep him from falling over things he could not see. The dog's name was Fan. She was big and strong and Lo-Sun became very fond of her, for she was the cleverest creature imaginable and could do all manner of tricks. She could walk on her hind legs, turn somersaults, lie down and pretend to be dead and then come to life and jump over a stick when Lo-Sun gave the word. She was a fine swimmer, too, and in the evenings, when Lo-Sun and his mother walked by the river, they used to throw a ball into the water and Fan would plunge in and fetch it out. As he grew older, Lo-Sun used often to go to the market in place of his mother, for Fan would let no one touch him or take anything that he was carrying.

So all went on until the year in which Lo-Sun became ten years old; and in that year, there came a pestilence over all that part of China. Thousands died and thousands more lost their livelihood, for work and trade fell away to nothing and people feared to venture any distance from their homes. And during that evil time Lo-Sun's mother sickened and died.

Now Lo-Sun's father had never shown him any love, or concealed his disappointment that his son was blind and therefore, in his eyes, worthless: and now that times were so hard and they could scarcely get even enough to eat, it was not long after his mother's death before he turned Lo-Sun out of the house and told him never to return. The poor boy wandered away across the city, helpless and friendless except for his faithful Fan. Without Fan he would have died on the streets; but she guided his footsteps, kept him from harm and with her clever tricks often attracted and pleased strangers and passers-by, so that they would give something to the poor blind boy: and in this way the two of them managed to survive. At night they would lie down together in whatever rough shelter the

dog could find, and as the weeks went by and the terrible sickness abated, Lo-Sun gradually became accustomed to the hard life of a beggar, and learned the ways in which the wretched and afflicted contrive to keep themselves alive.

Now one night, as he was sleeping in a doorway, pressed against Fan for warmth, Lo-Sun dreamed a strange dream. It seemed that he was standing in warm sunshine in some pleasant, open place, and could hear all around him the rustling of summer leaves, the murmur of bees and the scent of flowers. Then he heard footsteps approaching and a voice said, 'Lo-Sun, do you see me?'

'Alas, sir,' replied Lo-Sun, 'I am blind; but I can hear you.'

'I am a messenger of God,' said the voice, 'and this is His message. If only you have courage and determination enough, Lo-Sun, you can gain your sight; you can become your own healer. Henceforth, each time you do a good deed, no matter how small, a little light will reach your eyes, and at last, if only you persevere, you will come to see the whole world as clearly as anyone who has ever dwelt in it. But mark well, as often as you commit a bad or dishonest deed, so you will darken your own eyes.'

Lo-Sun waited in silence, but the voice said no more; and then, it seemed, the leaves and flowers around him faded, just as a scent dies on the air, and he returned into deep sleep.

Waking in the morning, cold and cramped on the hard stone, he remembered the dream. For a while he pondered it, recalling each detail of the place full of flowers and the strange voice, but then hunger drove it from his mind and he set out as usual through the streets.

That day was a hard and luckless one and by nightfall the poor lad had eaten little and been able to beg no more than two farthings – scarcely enough to buy himself a mouthful. On such days he used sometimes to go and knock at the back door of a kindly baker, who might – as long as it was not too often – let him have a stale loaf in return for whatever he could give. Fan knew the

way well enough, and they were just turning into the alley behind the baker's shop when Lo-Sun stumbled across the outstretched legs of a man sitting propped against the wall. At once the man cried out, 'Ah, kind sir, pray spare something for a poor blind man!'

'Friend,' replied Lo-Sun, 'I am blind like yourself.'

'Yet my misfortune is greater than yours,' said the other, 'for I am not only blind, but crippled and cannot even walk.'

At this Lo-Sun, with no thought but the natural pity which sprang up within him, gave the man his two farthings; and for half that night lay awake from hunger in a place known as the Beggars' Palace – an old, tumble-down temple long deserted and given over to the homeless and destitute.

Next day, as he and Fan were begging at a street corner not far from the river, he realized, all of a sudden, that in some strange way which he had never before experienced, he had become aware of the movements of people passing nearby. Wonderingly, he raised and moved his hand before his face; and, as its faint outline came and went, understood with excitement that he must indeed now possess some slight vestige of sight. That evening he came upon an old woman so weak from hunger that she could scarcely walk, and with the help of Fan supported her as far as the Beggars' Temple, where he shared with her his few miserable scraps of food.

Hunger woke him before dawn. The weather was mild and he determined to go out of the town to a certain village where once or twice in the past Fan's tricks had earned a little money. While going along the road he happened to step in a puddle and a few moments later realized that the momentary gleam in his eyes must have been the splash of water against the light. At this he turned back and stamped his foot in the puddle again. Then, sitting down by the roadside, he began picking leaves and blades of grass and holding them up before his eyes.

He became so deeply absorbed that for some time he did not notice that Fan had left his side, but as soon as he did so he sprang up in alarm and began calling her. Almost at once she returned and laid at his feet a hen which, as he felt its warm, limp body, he knew that she must just have killed. Afraid, he listened, trembling, for the angry voice of the owner; but all was quiet and no one came. Lo-Sun guessed that the hen must have strayed. If he took it to the town, he would be able to sell it for more money than he could hope to get in two or three days of begging. Tucking it out of sight under his ragged cloak, he hurried back and soon found a buyer in the market – a good-natured man who was not concerned to drive a hard bargain or ask awkward questions of a blind boy. No sooner had the money been counted into his hand than the dim twilight faded before his eyes and he realized, with a bitter pang, how much he had thrown away. He had forgotten, during the past two days, how dense had been that groping darkness into which he now found himself plunged once more.

For some time he sat silent in a corner of the market. Then, led by Fan, he made his way back to the village, where he inquired from house to house till he found the woman who owned the hen. He gave her the money, explaining only that his dog had killed the hen before he himself knew what it was about. The good woman was touched by his honesty and although she took the money, gave him a meal and a few pence for himself. That night he and Fan slept in an old barn on the edge of the village, and next morning he found that his eyes had once more begun to perceive traces of light.

Weeks passed. Autumn followed summer, and still Lo-Sun struggled on towards his mysterious goal. Many times he felt that hardship and loneliness would overwhelm him, and when things went badly, as all too often they did, he would be filled with a bitter resentment against the injustice of his cruel father. At such times he could discern no glimmer of light; and as he sat, miserably moving a stick or blade of grass to and fro before his eyes, he would silently entreat the spirit of his dream to grant him still more courage and determination.

At last, one rough, wet morning of early winter, as he woke to the sounds of the wind in the trees and the swollen river roaring between its banks, he found that he could not only make out the passers-by, but could actually tell men from women and young from old. In great joy he made his way to the shop of an old potter who had sometimes shown him kindness, and begged to be allowed to help him by sorting and arranging his pots for sale. He asked for no pay, but the potter, filled with wonder at the marvel of a blind boy who had partly gained his sight, invited him first to sit down and share his breakfast, and even found a bone for his clever dog.

That evening, when the potter had shut his shop and the sun was almost set, Lo-Sun was sitting on the river-bank, combing Fan with a jagged chip of wood and delightedly watching his own fingers pulling the burs and fragments of brambles out of her shaggy coat. Suddenly, not

far off, he heard a voice shout 'Look! A man has fallen into the river!'

The cry was taken up. People began running past him and all around he could hear shouts and calls as they watched the man struggling in the deep flood water. Close by, someone was being prevented by his friends from diving in to the rescue. 'The water's too rough,' they said. 'You'd only be throwing your life away! Anyway, in a few moments the poor fellow's bound to lose his hold on that bit of rock and be swept downstream.'

Lo-Sun led Fan to the brink of the river. All he could see was the brown, turbid water racing by at his feet, but now he could hear plainly the desperate cries of the man clinging to the rock a little way below. Giving himself no time to think that he was risking all he had in the world, he pushed Fan into the river and as she vanished from his sight stood shouting 'Fetch him, Fan, fetch him!' at the top of his voice.

People were crowding round.

'You stupid boy, all you've done is lose your dog!' said a voice.

'He meant well, all the same,' said another.

'Look, look, the dog's got him!' cried a man behind his back: and then it seemed as though hundreds of people were shouting and pushing forward and Lo-Sun, nearly knocked into the river, was forced to crouch down and clutch at the bushes to save himself.

'They're being swept down together!'

'The dog's got him! The dog's holding him up!'

'They'll never get to the other bank!'

'Yes, see, the man's ashore! Over there, look!'

'Where's the dog? What's happened to the dog?'

The crowd, still calling to one another, went running downstream and Lo-Sun was left alone on the bank. He tried to follow, calling out and entreating anyone who might hear to tell him what had happened, but no one paid him any attention. Thinking that he could see one of the men who had been close beside him while Fan

was swimming, he tried to follow him, calling out to him to stop. But without his dog he had no hope of catching up with the man and at last lost sight of him altogether; and then realized that he did not know where he was. It grew quite dark and the poor boy, weeping bitterly, sank down on a patch of waste ground and at length fell asleep.

When he woke next morning, his first feelings were of shock and fear, and his next to wonder where he could possibly be. The world had changed. There seemed to be people everywhere. Above their heads, the bare branches of trees were tossing in the wind. There were birds perching on the rooves and as he turned his head the sun shone full in his eyes and dazzled them. Blinking and staring about him, he understood that the distant, sliding mass of grey at the far end of the street must be the river. He could see – he could see as plainly as anyone else!

Slowly – for only gradually could he get used to what had happened – Lo-Sun made his way back to the bank and began asking everyone he met whether they could tell him what had become of the dog which had saved the man the night before. But the river was wide, the nearest ferry was two miles away and no one had heard any news from the other side. At last he gave up and went back to the potter's shop. When the potter had heard his story and proved for himself that the boy's sight was perfect, he could not contain his astonishment, but ran down the street to tell his brother, who worked at the inn near the Dragon Gate.

Lo-Sun was left sitting among the pots, grieving for poor Fan and wondering whether he dared ask the potter to take him on as an apprentice. Suddenly, a shadow fell across his eyes. Looking up, he saw in the doorway a man struggling to keep his balance as Fan, whom he was holding on a length of cord, almost dragged him bodily into the shop. With a cry of joy, Lo-Sun fell on his knees and clasped his beloved dog in his arms.

'My boy, do you know who I am?' asked the

stranger standing above him. Lo-Sun stood up, but could see only that the man's eyes were full of tears.

'Lo-Sun, I am your father,' said the man. 'It was I whose life you saved yesterday. When I recognized the dog, I knew who must have sent her into the flooded river when not a soul dared to come to my rescue. I have been searching the town to find you. Oh, my dear son, forgive me – I beg you, forgive my harshness and cruelty! Only come home with me, that I may show myself a true father and make amends to you for the wrong I have done!'

The potter and his brother, hastening back down the street, found Lo-Sun and his father embracing one another in speechless joy, while Fan jumped up to lick their faces. So the story ends happily, as all tales should; especially tales of good Chinese boys who honour their parents and act bravely and patiently, whatever trials life may bring.

Now gather up your playthings, my dear son, and be off to bed like a good lad; for see, here come four foreign devils with their shameless, painted trollops, and your dear father and I must be about some honest work. Good evening, sir. Good evening, madam. 'Nice to see you here again.

STAN BOLOVAN AND THE DRAGON

The boy Benson, up on the form! And anyone else acting in an anti-social manner
merely because it happens to be the last day of
term will – what, Roberts? Well, the penultimate
day, then. The barbarous festivities traditionally
indulged in on this day will not be conducted in
this classroom until I have been able to get a
decent distance away from it; and among those,
Randall, I include consumption of the toffee
which I observe you to be tentatively fingering.
Kindly return it to your pocket.

I am aware that examinations are over and that
a spirit of levity prevails in your minds, which it
would therefore be impossible to penetrate with
any real instruction, such as the conjugation of
'fio' or the missionary journeys of Saint Paul.
What was that, the boy Matthews? Even more
impossible than usual? It cannot be *more* impossible than usual, Matthews. A thing is either
impossible or else it isn't. If it's impossible it
can't be *more* impossible, can it? Either a jug of
milk's pure or it's not. It can't be purer than
another lot, whatever the advertisements say. It's
my unhappy job to endeavour to instil into your
minds – or what for the sake of decency we must
call your minds – some inkling of these matters.

Where was I? The boy Steel, where was I? Ah,

yes – it would be useless to try to impart instruction on 'fio' during the last *full* day of term, Roberts. How absolute the knave is. I therefore intend to tell you a story, and when I have finished I shall require you all to write a free composition, telling me what you consider to be the moral of the story and in what way – if at all – its sentiments may be held to be applicable today. You had better sit close; and Benson, you may now descend from that bad eminence to which you were by merit raised. The story will, of course, be an edifying one. What does 'edifying' mean, Bridges? No, it does *not* mean 'appetizing', though I had no doubt you'd say it did. Lock? Yes, quite right. It means that it will do you good. 'Edify' – literally 'to build', from 'aedifico, aedificare', first conjugation, like 'amo'. 'Balbus murum aedificavit'. All right, Tweedy, I know you can translate it, and so can everyone else. But more commonly, 'edify' means 'to instruct' or 'improve'.

He gave, he taught; and edified the more
Because he showed by proof 'twas easy to be poor.

This will be an improving story, and if it starts badly, perhaps it will improve as it goes on. That is a joke, tiny pupils. But to discover whether it does or not, you'll have to sit still, Benfield, won't you, and put away that matchbox, which no doubt contains some revolting insect that you intend to domesticate.

Once upon a time, many years ago, in Roumania, there lived a peasant named Stan Bolovan who, though small and weak, was extremely sharp in his wits. It was very seldom that anyone was able to cheat him. He'd kept his head above water for many years, even though at times he felt almost surrounded by people trying to get the better of him or pull tricks behind his back. He has my sympathy. He might very well have made enough to buy a farm of his own or set himself up in business in the town, but there was one great obstacle to any plan of that kind, and that was the very large size of his family. None of them was yet old enough to be any real help to

him about the place, but they all required food and clothing, and Stan Bolovan was usually at his wits' end to find enough to go round. In fact, most of the time, for all he was so sharp-witted, he couldn't manage it at all; and on top of that there was the house to be kept in repair and the horse and the dogs to be fed, and shoe leather to find, to say nothing of things like tools and domestic equipment, which don't go on for ever, as you'll no doubt be discovering for yourselves in a few years' time. One way and another, Stan Bolovan was badly troubled to know how to make ends meet, for his family always seemed to be clamouring for food; and one day he said to his wife, 'You know, my dear, there's no help for it, I'll just have to set off into the great world, see whether I can't make some money one way or another, and bring it back here. It's summer time, so you'll be able to manage for a while, at any rate. Whatever happens, I'll be home again before the winter and with any luck there'll be an end to all our worries. So just you put me up a bit of food, now, in a clean handkerchief, and give me my old stick and hat, and I'll be off; for the sooner I'm off, the sooner I'll be home again, you know.'

Well, Mrs Bolovan put him up a bit of bread, a few apples and a large, round cream cheese, which was about all she had to spare, and off went Stan on his travels, with no very clear idea of exactly what he meant to do. He walked and walked until he came to the last land before the edge of Nowhere and there, one fine evening at sunset, he sat down on a great, flat stone by the road and fell to wondering, not for the first time, what sort of a shift he was going to try. He'd eaten the bread and the apples and now all he had left was the half of the cream cheese, which he was trying to make last as long as possible.

Now as he sat there, with his heart in his boots and like enough to run out through the holes in the leather, he noticed a fine flock of sheep grazing on the hillside opposite, and a herd of cows in the meadow below them. Near-by stood a very poor-looking farmhouse, the roof all sagging and the gate in the wall badly in need of a coat of paint, as anyone could see.

'I wonder whether they could do with a bit of help?' thought Stan. 'If only I could get a square meal and a roof over my head, I might be able to see the next jump ahead. I'll give it a try, anyway.'

So off he went to the farmhouse and knocked on the door, and when the farmer came out he asked him for a job.

'Are you mad?' asked the farmer, looking him up and down. 'Didn't anyone warn you to keep away from here if you value your life?'

At this Stan wondered whether the farmer might be some sort of a friend of Boris Karloff and going to do him in, but it didn't seem very

likely, because he looked so gaunt and worried, as though he were frightened half out of his wits. So Stan asked him what there was to be afraid of.

'It's the dragon,' answered the farmer, 'as everyone knows for miles around. That there dragon's already eaten up the stock of twenty farms this side of Nowhere, and now he's eating up the stock of this one as well. It used to be a fine farm, but it won't last long now the dragon's started on it. I tell you, unless you want to be killed you'd better be off.'

'Why do you stay here, then?' asked Stan Bolovan, thinking to himself that it was no wonder the place looked so much in need of repair.

'That's the worst of the whole thing,' answered the farmer bitterly. 'The dragon's taken away my poor wife to work for his old mother in their cave up the mountain, and he swears that if I go away he'll kill her and hang up her bones in the trees. I've been living here alone now these three months, looking after the beasts and doing what he tells me. He comes every night and takes three or four sheep and as many cows. There's no way to get the better of him, believe you me.'

'I see,' said Stan. 'Yes, that must make life

extremely awkward. Well, now, suppose I were to rid you of this dragon for good and all, what would you give me?'

'I'd like to see you do it first,' said the farmer, and went in and shut the door, for he thought that Stan Bolovan must be making fun of him.

It was now after sunset, and Stan was turning away down the lane when suddenly he heard a tremendous rushing noise in the air. Next moment the last light in the sky was obscured by a great, flying mass as big as a church. Stan Bolovan crouched down behind the wall and as he did so the dragon alighted in the field and immediately proceeded to kill three sheep and three cows. The smoke of his breath scorched the leaves on the nearest trees and his tail, which he was lashing from side to side, happened to knock down the length of wall behind which Stan was hiding. He was lucky not to be damaged by the falling stones. The dragon saw him at once, in spite of the bad light, and came across the field in a single leap.

'What do you think you're doing here?' he roared, poking his head through the broken wall and glaring down at Stan Bolovan lying on his back among the stones. 'Don't you know this is my farm and these are my beasts?'

'I'll tell you who I am,' replied Stan Bolovan, getting to his feet and looking him squarely in the eye – for he knew that it would be fatal to show any fear. 'I'm Stan Bolovan the Dauntless, who milks rocks for supper and eats them too. I'm a one-man wave of destruction. I shave with a blow-lamp. I clean my teeth with iron filings and cut my nails with a circular saw. And if I have any lip from you –'

'Now, just a moment, buster,' said the dragon. 'Just a moment. What do you mean, you milk rocks for supper? That's not a question of strength. There's no milk in rocks, you stupid little man.'

'There most certainly is,' replied Stan Bolovan. 'It's simply that a fool like you can't tell good rocks from bad ones, that's all. For instance, this rock I've just put into my bag is exactly the kind I need. If you knew enough to tell peas from turnips you'd know the sort you ought to be looking for. It wouldn't make any difference, though. *You* couldn't squeeze any milk out of a rock if you tried for a week. Call yourself a dragon? Why –'

At this the dragon grabbed a rock and squeezed it as hard as he could, while Stan Bolovan opened his bag and took out his pannikin and the half of the cream cheese – which was rather grubby with being at the bottom of the bag and in the twilight looked very like a stone.

'Now you watch this,' said he, and squeezed the cheese so that the buttermilk ran dripping out into the pannikin. The dragon, who had never seen a cream cheese in his life, watched in astonishment. Stan Bolovan handed him the pannikin and, while he was licking it, ate the remains of the cheese before the dragon could get a closer look.

'Well, I'll just be getting along now,' he said, 'but I'm warning you, if you come back here or give my farmer friend any more trouble, I'll squeeze your neck harder than that stone, until your silly eyes pop out.'

'Wait a minute,' said the dragon. 'How would you like to come and work for me and my old mother, up in our cave? I've got a lot of treasure up there and I'll pay you very well indeed.' But he was really thinking that if once he could get Stan up in the air on his back, he'd throw him down and kill him.

Stan thought about it quickly and decided that danger or not, this seemed the only chance likely to come his way of making his fortune.

'Very well,' he said, 'but I can't come tonight. I've promised to go and bend some iron bars for a friend who's making a cattle-pen. If I just put them across my knee, you know, it saves paying the blacksmith. I'll be with you tomorrow evening. I know where to come, because I jumped over the mountain on my way here, so you needn't bother to fly down for me.' And with that he strolled away.

He spent the following day climbing the mountain and a long job it was, through woods and over rocks in the hot, dry weather. When at last he saw the dragon's cave in the distance, he crouched down, took out his matches and set some of the grass and bushes alight. As soon as they were burning well he rubbed ash on his face and coat and then singed his sleeve with a smouldering stick. A few moments later, just as he'd expected, he saw the dragon coming to find out what was making the smoke. As the dragon came up, he began beating at his clothes, stamping his feet and muttering 'What a nuisance! This always happens in dry weather. I shan't have a coat left soon.'

'What on earth have you been up to?' asked the dragon, beating out the fire with his great, leathery tail.

'I'm sorry,' replied Stan, 'I really should have thought. It's not the first time this sort of thing's happened, I'm afraid. I was a bit late starting out to come here, so I ran up the mountain. I was going fairly fast and unfortunately I set the bushes alight as I came through them. Scorched my coat too – most annoying. It's good of you to have put the fire out, but you needn't have bothered: I was just going to spit on it. Anyway, let's get on to your cave.'

When they reached the dragon's cave, the first thing Stan saw was the poor farmer's wife, chained up to the wall and scouring away at a couple of great iron pots.

'Well, you won't be needing *her* any more, now you've got me,' he said. 'She can just get off home. Never mind if you can't find the key for the chain. I can easily bite it through at the shackle end.' And he picked it up.

'Stop! Stop!' shouted the dragon. 'That's a valuable chain – the only one we've got. I took it off a gallows last year. Just you let it alone and I'll unlock it myself.'

The farmer's wife was off out of the cave as fast as she could go and while Stan was outside, showing her the best way down the mountain,

the dragon went and woke up his old mother, who was asleep in the back kitchen.

'Listen, mother,' he said. 'This man I was telling you about – he's turned up. I promised him a lot of treasure to get him here so that we could kill him off nice and quiet, in his sleep. Frankly, I'm afraid to tackle him any other way. He's a one-man wave of destruction. He shaves with a blow-lamp, he cleans his teeth –' Allsop! There is no need to roll about and laugh in that immoderate and vulgar manner. If you wish to hear the rest of this story and not to be sent out of the room, kindly contain yourself. Where was I?

'Pooh!' said the old mother dragon, 'you always were a great fool. Just you leave him to me. I'm certainly not going to kill him in his sleep. It's very bad style for dragons, is that; as though we were afraid of him, or something. I'll show you how to fix him fair and square, you see if I don't.'

Stan was given a sleeping-place of his own at the back of the dragon's cave; and the next morning he went out into the forest and began cutting firewood. He'd got quite a nice bit together when the dragon and his mother came out to where he was working. The dragon was carrying a polished club the size of a goal-post cross-bar, with an asbestos-mounted silver plaque on the handle which said, 'Draconian Sports Association. Field Events Championship Award. Won outright in the Year of the Green Dragon.'

'See that?' asked the dragon rather unnecessarily, throwing it down so that the leaves fell off the nearest trees and Stan Bolovan's backbone vibrated like a double-bass string. 'Club-throwing champion of Lacertilia and Neuropteron; three years running. How far do you think *you* can throw it?'

'I'll see you throw it first,' answered Stan. 'I wouldn't want to damage it – seeing it's of sentimental value.'

'Oh, a contest, is it?' said the dragon. 'Very well, excellent. And if I win, you'll just forfeit your head, my man.'

Thereupon the dragon picked up the club in his tail, whirled it round a few times and threw it out of sight.

'I'll put you up a bit of a picnic, dear, and you can go and find it,' said his mother. 'That's the worst of these field events – there's such a lot of time between one bit of action and the next. Still, you've got a nice day for it.'

As Stan still refused to fly on the dragon's back, it took them all day to get to where the club was lying. The sun had just set, the moon was rising behind them and the club was sticking up out of a field of wheat with red poppies in it. Without a word, Stan sat down on the bank with his chin in his cupped hands and remained staring steadily at the eastern skyline.

'Well, hurry up and throw it,' said the dragon. 'What are you waiting for?'

'I'm waiting for the moon to rise higher and get out of the way,' answered Stan. 'If the club were to stick in the moon, you wouldn't get it back and that'd be a pity – a nice, presentation club like that. Still, if you're in a hurry –'

He got up and spat on his hands.

'Wait, wait!' said the dragon. 'Just a minute! what makes you think you could throw it into the moon?'

'Because that's what happened last time,' said Stan. 'D'you see that dark hole up there, on the right side of the moon? That was a boulder, actually, that I threw last year, when I was in China – but it's all the same, you know.'

'You'd better not throw it at all,' said the dragon, sulkily. 'I don't want to risk losing it. We'll just take it home again.'

'What about the treasure you promised me?' asked Stan. 'When do I get paid?'

'Oh, later, later,' said the dragon. 'I'll – er – see you about that in a few days' time. See you further,' he muttered under his breath, and took off for home without another word.

Stan Bolovan took care not to get back to the cave until two mornings later, not wishing to sleep there if he could help it. He was still very much frightened of the dragon, but he'd also come to realize that intelligence was not the strongest of dragon qualities and he was determined to get his hands on some of the treasure at least, even though it meant continuing to risk his life.

He found the dragon just setting out to draw water from a stream half a mile below the cave. He had two colossal iron pails, as big as pianos, strapped on his back.

'Ah, there you are,' said the dragon. 'About time too. You can come and give me a hand filling these. The cave's got low on water. We use a good deal, you know, one way and another.'

It was on the tip of Stan's tongue to ask 'What for?' – the cave being about as clean and tidy as the inside of Eccleston's desk – silence, Eccleston! – but he thought better of it and followed the dragon down to the spring. Stan unstrapped the pails and the dragon filled them both in a moment. Then he flew to the cave, first with one and then with the other, emptied each into the cistern and brought them both back. As he alighted, he found Stan Bolovan marking out the ground with a pointed stick on either side of the stream.

'What on earth are you doing now?' asked the dragon.

'Got a spade?' replied Stan. 'Just go and get it for me, will you?'

'Whatever for?'

'Well, you obviously haven't realized that you could save yourself all this work by simply digging up the stream and taking it to the cave. You're lucky to have an expert like me, you really are. Of course, I'll have to charge you for specialist advice. To digging up one stream, £1. To knowing how, £999. It's very cheap at that price, actually. The one I did for the King of Armenia cost a lot more than that, but it was a bigger one, of course. It runs through the palace gardens now. You might like to go and have a look at it some time.'

'But I don't want the stream running through the cave,' shouted the dragon. 'Think of the mess, and all the mud in winter –'

'Nonsense,' said Stan firmly. 'Anyway, it's only this bit here I'm going to dig up. You'll like it when you've got it. Now just go and get the spade like a good fellow –'

'No, I'm darned if I will,' said the dragon. 'Please – I beg you – do give up this idea. We're just plain folk here. It wouldn't suit me and my mother at all.'

'Oh, all right,' replied Stan. 'But I really must draw the line at all this ridiculously old-fashioned water-carrying. I'll just have a nap and you can let me know when you've finished.' And with that he lay down. But he only pretended to go to sleep; for he always remained very much on his guard with the dragon, whom he didn't trust an inch.

That afternoon, after a revolting meal of rancid mutton and onions, the dragon's mother sent them off to collect firewood from a grove near the foot of the mountain, the dragon explaining that he preferred not to fell the trees near the cave, for the sake of cover and shelter from the wind.

'Now, you watch this,' said he, and thereupon proceeded to fell five trees with one blow of his tail. As they came crashing down, he tied them into a bundle with a length of rope as thick as Stan's arm.

Stan looked at the bundle and shrugged his shoulders.

'I can save you all that work, you know,' he said. 'That's really a very antiquated method of winning timber. Go back and bring me that chain, can you – the one you used for the farmer's wife?'

'Whatever are you going to do with that?' asked the dragon nervously.

'Well, when I was working on cedars for the Emperor of Ethiopia, I just used to chain a thousand trees together, pull out the lot and drag them up to the royal workshops. The king got rather cross, actually – 'said I'd left no cedars at all, you know. I told him he ought to have thought of that before he engaged a man like me.

Only you get a bit carried away when they all come toppling down like ninepins – 'kind of goes to your head.'

'I don't think you'd better do that here,' said the dragon. 'We need some trees left for next year –'

'Oh, no,' said Stan, marking a few suitable trees with his knife, 'you'll soon get used to a nice, open hillside. Cowslips, you know, buttercups –'

'To blazes with buttercups!' yelled the dragon. 'You just let those trees alone! We'll go home with what we've got.'

'Very well,' said Stan. 'Suit yourself. It's your forest.'

That night Stan excused himself and went to bed early, but he didn't go to sleep, because he felt sure the dragon would be after him, one way or another. It was easy to stay awake, because the supper had been so dreadful that he'd hardly been able to eat anything. He waited a bit and then crept out of his room, which was a sort of hollow in the rock, and tiptoed along on the sand until he was just round the corner from the main part of the cave. After a bit, sure enough, the dragon got up, switched off the dragovision and said, 'Look here, mother, we've simply *got* to do away with this Stan man. You say it's bad style for dragons to kill men in their sleep, but any port in a storm. There's no getting the better of him any other way, that's plain. He's a one-man wave –'

'I've heard all that,' says she. 'But as a matter of fact, I think you're right, son. You'd better just wait an hour till he's off really sound, and then take your club and finish him. I'd be ashamed for any of the other dragons to learn we'd been pushed to that, though. 'Better keep quiet about it.'

Stan nipped back to bed wondering how on earth he was going to manage this time. He'd half a mind to cut and run, but the thought of the treasure and all his hungry children made him think better of it. It wouldn't be good enough just to be out of bed when the dragon arrived. He had to think of a trick worth two of that. After some time he went out round the back of the cave, and here he found an old pig-trough lying under a tree in the moonlight. He picked it up as quietly as he could, carried it indoors and put it in his bed. Then he filled it up with earth and put his coat over it, and the blankets over that, and stuck a turnip at the top for a head. After that, he hid under the bed and tried to do a bit of realistic snoring.

Sure enough, after a bit in crept the dragon with his prize club, groped around a bit and then proceeded to spoil the pig-trough for good and all – bash, bash. It didn't take long, and when the dragon had gone chuckling away in the dark, Stan came out and dismantled his handiwork, although he took good care to wait a long time before carrying what was left of the trough outside and hiding it in the wood.

In the morning he made his bed and then went out and asked the dragon if he could have some hot water to wash. The dragon stared at him open-mouthed and then asked whether he'd slept well.

'Oh, well enough,' replied Stan, 'only I seem to have a bit of a headache, for some reason. I dare say it'll pass off. Well now, I wonder what you'd like me to do today? I've been thinking, you know, that if I were just to pull down one side of this cave, let a bit of light in –'

'No, no,' cried the dragon, 'that wouldn't suit us at all! Make a new plan, Stan! In fact, if only you'll go home, you shall have as much treasure as you like to take with you. What we need round here is a bit of peace.'

'But how on earth am I to carry it away?' asked Stan, off his guard for a moment with delight.

'Oh, I thought you'd just carry it away under your arm,' replied the dragon, bitterly. 'I mean, no trouble for you, what?'

'I think I'll have to ask *you* to carry it for me,' said Stan. 'It would really be beneath my dignity to be seen carrying sacks of gold about. Where I come from we have animals to do that. Besides, I couldn't really settle for less than thirty sacks, and that might be rather a lot to carry, even for me.'

So off they went, Stan walking in front and the poor dragon trudging along behind with the gold on his back, like a donkey. As they were approaching Stan's home, his eldest son saw him coming and the whole family came pouring out, shouting, 'Dad! Dad! Did you get anything? We haven't had a decent meal since you left!'

'Fancy a bit of dragon?' said Stan. 'I dare say he'll be rather tough, but it'll make a change, anyway. Hang on a minute.' And he took out his old knife.

At this the dragon threw down the thirty sacks of gold with a howl, spread his wings and took to the air as fast as he could. And if he hasn't come down yet, I dare say he's flying still.

'Well,' said Stan to the children as they stood staring after him, 'to tell you the truth, he would have been a good deal too tough. I'll take you all down to the Chinese restaurant instead.' And so he did.

Now take out your pens – that includes you, Andrewes; come on, wretched boy, make haste – and a sheet of paper each – Surely that can't be the bell? Dear me, I fear you will have to be disappointed. Taylor! Last day of term or first day of term, I have repeatedly told you that you do *not* jump up and dash for the door the moment you hear the bell. When everyone is sitting down in a composed and properly-controlled manner, I will dismiss the class. I hope you all have pleasant holidays. Where am I going, Denman, did you ask? I am going walking in north Scotland. 'Ubi solitudinem faciunt, pacem appellant.' Johnson? Morgan? Never mind. We will leave it for next term.

THE CROW
=AND THE=
DAYLIGHT

That'll be enough of those bigger logs for today, lad. That whole pile there adds up to a good stock – what, two hundred, two hundred and fifty, wouldn't you think? I can sell that lot easily – more, probably, but that'll do for now. Then those short lengths and rough pieces lying there, we'll just take them across and pile them along the side of the road, over yonder; then when your dad comes back with the car, we can fill up the trunk. That'll make a nice bit of burning for all of you at home. Now you just take the bill-hook and trim the small branches off, while I sit down on this log and have a smoke. Lazy man, eh? Well, when you're an uncle with a nephew of your own, you can do the same: there's a bargain for you! Is the safety-catch on the gun? Good – just lean it up against there, then.

Ah, now, when I was a lad your age, many was the load of wood I had to drag home with nothing but my two hands. Sometimes on a sledge, but mostly on my back or even just along the ground. Well, yes, it *was* a hard life, there's no saying it wasn't, and I'm glad enough you haven't got the same. In those days we counted ourselves lucky to get wood any way at all.

The old Esquimau life will soon be a thing of the past, and I'm not one to shed any tears about that, for often enough it was more than hard. An Esquimau who's had the sense to come south is a wise man, my lad, and an Esquimau who's become an American citizen is wiser still. No, no! Take the axe to that bigger branch – no good chipping away with the bill-hook. Right, that's the style.

The further south the better, I say. More daylight and more civilization. St Michael was better than Barrow, and Dillingham's better than St Michael. 'Stands to reason – there's a thousand miles between Dillingham and Barrow, so they tell me. But I wouldn't go further south – not into Canada, nor into the Aleutians either. What would be the good of that? Your father and I, we've travelled enough; and your mother and your aunt too. Folk have got to settle down some time.

Ah, shoot, as the American engineer says, that's my last match! Oh, you've got a box? Good boy! I'll just have to turn my back to this breeze to get a light.

Good God, lad, you made me jump! What the devil are you at? Just pick up the gun and blaze off without a word of warning! Made me drop my pipe! Next time I'll take a stick to you, that I will! What were you firing at? A crow? You fired at a *crow*? Thank God you missed it! Don't you know better than to shoot at a crow? Just you give that gun to me. I'll hang on to it.

'No-good birds', did you say? What sort of Yankee talk is that? Is that what they teach you at that Yankee school your father sends you to? You're no true Esquimau, my boy, that's plain. Now you just listen to me, for I'm serious. No Esquimau ever harms a crow, do you understand? Do you want to bring bad luck on the lot of us, just when things are going well at last? No Esquimau ever kills a crow – the bird of good fortune – I don't care how many Cadillacs your father's bought.

'Why?' do you ask? What ignorance! Just you lay down that bill-hook now, and I'll tell you why, while we carry these logs across to the road-side there. They'll do – you've trimmed them off enough to fit into the trunk of the car.

My grandfather first told me the tale when I was only a little boy, hardly more than a baby. That was up in Barrow, but he was a true Esquimau, for he told me *his* grandfather was born on Victoria Island, and that's a thousand miles to the east, so he said. Ay, he used to watch the seal-holes in the ice, eight hours at a stretch and longer, with his feet in a leather thong to still the trembling! There was a hard life for a man! Yet once, long ago, it was harder still, and would be now if it wasn't for the crow. Wait and I'll tell you.

Long ago, then, before there were any white men from one end of this land to the other, there was no daylight in all Alaska, nor yet in the lands to the north. That's what my old grandfather said. 'Twas all darkness, from one end of the country to the other, and in that darkness the Esquimaux lived, just doing the best they could. They used to quarrel, sometimes, over whether it was day or night. Half the people slept while the other half worked. No one knew when it was time to go to bed or when it was time to get up, because it was dark all the time. 'Must have been a real mess, eh?

Now in one Esquimau village there lived a crow, just like that one you missed, thank God. The Esquimaux all liked this crow, because he was a cheeky fellow and used to fly in and out of their homes and make them laugh. What with it being so dark all the time and the crow being so

black, they never knew where he'd be next, so he got to hear all the gossip, and used to tell it up and down the village until everyone was in fits. No secrets in that village, you can be sure of that. And he was very wise, too. They knew that all right, for he'd told them so himself. And besides that, he used to tell them of all the wonderful lands he'd been to on his distant flights and long journeys to the east and the south.

Now one evening – one dark evening, or it might have been a dark morning, for the matter of that – the crow had just flown back from some expedition or other, and as he sat up in the light of the seal-oil lamp in the men's meeting-house, they could tell he seemed sad and out of spirits. So they said, 'What's the matter, crow? Why are you sad?'

'Why,' answers the crow, 'I feel sorry for all the Esquimau people, because they have no daylight.'

'Daylight?' they all asked him. 'What's that? What does it look like?'

'Well,' says the crow, cocking his head and looking round very sharp at them all, 'if you had daylight here in the north, you'd be able to go wherever you liked and see all you wanted; yes, even animals when they were far away. You'd be well off.'

So then they fell to asking him whether he couldn't go and bring them back some of this daylight. But the crow replied that he couldn't.

'It's too far to go,' he said. 'Much too far. Mind you, I know where it is, but it's a long way and I'd never be able to carry the daylight back here. Besides, they'd never give it to me. I should have to steal it, and a very dangerous business that would be.'

Then they all came crowding round – treading on each other's toes because of the bad light – and begged and entreated him to go to the place where the daylight was and bring them some back. The chief said, 'Oh, crow, you're so brave and clever, we know you can do it; if only you'll go, we'll honour you and your children for ever, until the end of time.'

Put that awkward-shaped log just there, boy, and then wedge it with the other one to stop it rolling. That's the way. Now stack this one behind it. Good.

So at last the crow said he would go; but he warned them that he might very well be a long time coming back, if indeed he ever managed to come back at all. And the next day he started out on his journey, flying away to the east; and how he knew the direction I can't say, but I dare say he may have gone by the stars. He flew on and on until he was exhausted, but he couldn't stop anywhere for long, partly because of the darkness and partly because of the cold.

Well, after many days he began to see a little light ahead of him, and then more and more, until at last the sky was full of sunshine. Now he was able to stop and rest, and he looked all about to see where the light was coming from; for this was a strange country to him, and even though he'd told the Esquimaux that he knew where the daylight was, he really had very little idea of how to go about the job he'd taken on. There were still no trees – only the snow and ice – so as he had nothing but the ground to perch on, he couldn't see very far.

At last he thought that the daylight seemed to be coming from a big snow-house in a village not far off; so he flew towards it and spent some time looking all around. And as he was puzzling over what to do next, suddenly there came a great flood of light which quite dazzled him. When he got his sight back, he saw that the door of the big house had opened and there was a beautiful girl standing in the doorway with a pail, and she was talking and waving to someone inside. From the way she was talking, the crow thought it must be a baby. After a few more moments she went off towards the ice-hole in the river, to fetch water, and while she was gone the crow plucked up his courage and came right up to the daylight house. 'Now,' thinks he, 'I'll just have to make a start and see what can be done. It'll be a ticklish job, I dare say.'

And with that, he slipped out of his skin, hid it

under a pile of soft snow round the back and began to sing a crow-charm. Now the whole point of this was that it came more slowly out of both sides of his mouth than the other, spinning seven threads round the inside-out of yesterday and under the lining of last year's dawn at midnight – just where the flame goes when the lamp's put out, you know. That's to make it simple, but it was a lot tighter than that's long, all the same.

> Louder than moonlight and redder than grey,
> Take off my shadow and tuck it away.
> No one can touch me the harder he tries,
> Nobody hear me without any eyes.

There was a great deal more to this than nothing in a full pocket, but you wouldn't understand if I wasn't to tell you something else and rather less, so I can't hang it up on the floor for fear anyone should climb up it three months last big bear's birthday and boil the sea with a fish-hook. But the crow got smaller and smaller, till in the end he was just a little speck of dust floating in a golden sunbeam outside the door of that house. And after a time the chief's daughter, that's to say the beautiful girl, she came back with her pail of water and the crow just floated into her black hair and got carried into the house where the daylight was.

Inside, it was as bright as bright could be, and that wasn't surprising either, for as soon as his eyes got used to it the crow could see that there were a great many daylights there, some big and some small, all lodged high up and out of the way in different places. And on the floor there was a baby boy, and he was playing with all manner of little carved toys – dogs, foxes, bears, seals and kayak canoes – which his father had made for him out of walrus ivory. The girl picked the baby up and began talking to him and kissing him, and as she did so the little speck of dust drifted out of her hair and lighted on the baby's ear.

When the girl put the baby down again and went to do her cooking, he began to cry and whimper. So the girl came and picked him up

again and made a fuss of him, and then she said, 'What do you want? I'll give you anything. You're my beautiful boy,' and all such nonsense as women say to their babies and little ones. So then the crow whispered in the baby's ear, 'Ask for the daylight; ask for the daylight to play with.' Then the baby stretched out his hands and cried for the daylight, but most of the daylights in the house were too big and heavy, and in the end the girl fetched him down a small, round one to play with. It was just as bright as the others, but small enough for the baby to roll along the floor.

All the time, the crow was wondering how he was going to be able to grab hold of the daylight, because it was so smooth and hard. And at last he had the idea of whispering to the baby to roll it under the cupboard, where he couldn't get it out, and then to cry for his mother to come and get it out for him. After this had happened several times, the girl tied a string on the daylight, so that the baby could pull it out by himself.

As soon as he saw her do this, the crow just blew away off the baby's ear and lodged himself near the door. And soon he heard the baby's father, who was the chief of that village, coming back from hunting. As soon as the chief opened the door, the crow floated out in the draught of warm air, found his skin and turned himself back into his own size and shape. Then, when he'd made quite sure that there was no one about to see him, he began carrying snow up to the roof in his beak until he had a pile of it. After this he went down and began pecking and tapping on the door.

'What's making that noise?' the chief asked his wife, looking up from his supper.

'Why,' said she, 'it's nothing – only the wind.'

But the crow went on tapping, and at last the chief told his wife to go out and see what was making the noise. When he heard her coming the crow flew back up to the roof, and as soon as she looked out of the door he pushed the pile of snow so that it slid down and fell all over her head and shoulders. And while she still couldn't

see anything, he started pecking her hands and ears.

'Help! Help!' she cried, shaking her head and spluttering in the snow. 'There's some creature attacking me! Help!'

At that the chief got up and came running out, and in all the confusion the crow darted through the open door, grabbed the daylight by the string and was off like a flash of black lightning, the way he'd come. The chief and his wife saw him, of course, and raised a great outcry, so that all the village people came running out and shouting. Some of them shot arrows after him, but the crow kept dodging and whirling in the air and very soon he was out of sight, except for the shining of the daylight like a star in the distance.

On the way back he had an easier time of it altogether, for the daylight kept him warm and he could see where he was going. When he got near Alaska he thought he'd just try the daylight to see how it worked, so as he passed over the first village he scratched a piece of the brightness off and it fell down and lit the place up no bounds. So after that he did the same at every village he came to, until at last he got back to the one where he lived. And there he hovered right over the chief's house and dropped the daylight so that it burst all into little bits that scattered everywhere.

The people came crowding out, all staring about them, for they'd never seen anything the like of that. For a long time they couldn't make out what had happened at all, and then, all of a sudden, somebody shouted, 'Look, that's our crow up there in the sky! I can see him all that way off, just as he said we'd be able to!'

'Well, who ever would have thought it!' said the chief. 'Crow, come down, so that we can give you a feast!'

And so Crow came down, and they made him guest of honour at such a feast as none of them had ever had in their lives before. They were just finishing the last of it when suddenly one of them called out, 'Crow! It's getting dark again! What's happened? Don't tell us there's a catch in it! Is the daylight going to melt?'

'No, no!' answers Crow. 'Don't worry. It'll still get dark sometimes, but then the daylight will come back again. That's good-quality daylight, that is. That won't wear out between now and the end of the world.'

'Why does it still have to get dark, then?' they asked.

'Well, you see,' says Crow, 'if I'd been able to steal the big daylight, it would never get dark at all, even in winter; but the big daylight would have been much too heavy to carry. In this world you've got to take what you can get.'

And with that he stretched out and went to sleep.

And from that day to this everyone in Alaska knows better than to harm a crow, and if your father hasn't taught you that, I'd better just have a word with him, else he'll lose all he's gained if you start getting up to any of those silly gun tricks. Just you shake the crumbs out of the dinner bag, where that crow can find them when he comes back. That's it. Is that your father coming up the road now? 'Doesn't look like – oh, that's his Volkswagen, is it? I see; I just thought he'd be bringing the Cadillac, I don't know why. Cars – cars. Proper Yankee lad you're getting. I wouldn't wonder if your legs didn't fall off, one of these days. Well, the Volkswagen'll have to do, I suppose. I dare say there'll be room enough for a good few logs in the trunk.

THE ROCKS OF
KORSAN

Erik, come over here, where I'm sitting. Now, tell me, what were you doing earlier this evening? Driving the cows home, yes. And feeding the chickens, yes, I know that. And then you went down to the village to return the hedging gloves to old Mr Borgen. Ah, now tell me a little more. Yes, you met Knud and Hans in the road. And what were the three of you doing in the road? Playing – what sort of playing? Who else was there?

I think you *do* remember. You met – yes, you met Jarl, didn't you? You say it was just in fun? Do you think *he* thought that? Never mind how I know. You were teasing him and making fun of his withered arm, weren't you?

I dare say you *didn't* mean to be unkind. All the same, Jarl was hurt as much as though you'd meant to be as unkind as you could. You and the other boys managed to make him feel that he was ugly and that you didn't want him to be a friend of yours. There were three of you, weren't there? Otherwise he might very well have made you sorry, withered arm or no withered arm. I'm ashamed of you.

Well, don't cry; that won't do any good to you or anyone else. The best thing you can do will be to go and find Jarl tomorrow and tell him you're sorry. There's more to it than that, though. You've got a lot to learn. People aren't always worse than you – or me either – because they happen to be disfigured or afflicted. They have God's work to do, as we all have. And those who are so foolish or cruel as to treat them badly may very well find themselves ending up like the storks who angered their lord.

Well, I've done scolding you now, my boy. I know you're a good lad at heart. It was thoughtless and stupid, but no worse. You'll grow up to do better, no danger. Now dry your eyes, fetch your supper out of the kitchen and sit here with me, by the window. I'll tell you the story about the storks. Then you'll understand.

Long ago, they say, all the storks had fine tails – plumed like the grey crane and even finer than that. In those days they built their nests on the rooves of every city in Denmark – Kjöbenhavn and Odense, Hjörring, Aarhus and many more – for in those days there were fewer people and less noise. But they flew north every year, just as they do now – they flew north to attend the court of their lord, and they returned again in due season. The storks have always had a lord, who holds court each year – beyond Lake Enara in Finland, people say, though that I can't tell, for I was never up in those parts. But thousands upon thousands of storks have always assembled there, and brought news to their lord from all over the world, wherever they've flown. It's said that the stork lord has always been a powerful worker of magic; and storks are lucky, you

know, and bring good fortune to those who treat them well and leave their nests in peace.

Now once, in the far-off days of which I'm speaking, it happened that the king of Denmark's daughter was mortally injured while she was out riding in the woods. Her horse, a new one to which she wasn't accustomed, took fright and bolted among the trees, and before the princess was thrown she was terribly lacerated and pierced by the branches. She was carried back to the palace bleeding and unconscious, and the best doctors in the kingdom were summoned to her bedside. But there was little they could do for her, and within the hour they told the king that they could hold out no hope of her recovery. Both the king and queen were overwhelmed with grief, for she was their only child, very beautiful and just of an age to marry. The king had it proclaimed throughout the land that a fortune would be paid to anyone who could save her life, but none could be found to attempt a task which everyone knew to be beyond mortal powers.

Now there were two storks who had built their nest on the palace roof; and they, of course, had seen all that had happened and heard the king and queen weeping in the royal bedchamber. And as evening was falling, they flew down and tapped at the window until the king opened it.

'O king,' they said, 'if you will promise to give all storks throughout the land your blessing and protection, and order your subjects to treat them well for ever, we are ready to fly at once to the lord of the storks, in his court beyond Lake Enara, and tell him of your trouble. He is wise and powerful, and news reaches him from every land. If there's any remedy on earth by which the princess can be healed, he will know of it.'

The king, though he hardly dared to place any hope in the offer, agreed to what the two storks proposed, and at once they set out and flew northward night and day until they came to their lord's court. Here they found many storks gathered, for the lord and his council were busy hearing messengers and bringers of news from

India to Morocco, and Moscow to the Scheldt. The two storks, weary and hungry as they were, pushed their way forward and begged the lord's chamberlain to let them deliver their message, explaining that it was a matter of the greatest urgency.

When the stork lord had heard their news, he sat for some time in grave silence, shaking his head and pondering. At last he said, 'If the king's daughter is indeed dying of her injuries, the business is almost beyond hope, as the doctors have said. Here, in this court, we learn of all wisdom and skills known throughout the world, both to men and to beasts and birds – at least, wherever storks fly. There is only one hope for the king's daughter to be healed of such injuries, and that is a slender hope indeed. If some creature could journey to the world's end and bring back some of the water of death and the water of life, by those – and by those only – she could be restored.'

'But, my lord,' replied the chamberlain, 'there cannot be a bird in the world who would undertake such a mission. It would be certain death, for those waters spring up between the Rocks of Korsan.'

The two storks who had brought the king's message at once asked their lord to tell them of those Rocks and of the waters that rose between them, and offered to make the journey themselves. But when they had learned the nature of the place, whose very name struck fear into the hearts of all creatures who knew what manner of region it was, they were glad enough when the lord said he would not take them at their word. 'Though, thank God, I never saw those Rocks myself,' said he, 'yet I have spoken with some of the very few who have done so and returned alive. They stand on the further shore of a great sea, among an icy wilderness of islands at the end of the world, and between them lies a sheer ravine, a thousand feet deep yet no more than ten feet across. At the bottom of that ravine rise two springs, side by side. One yields the water of death and the other the water of life. The first, poured over a dead body, mends all broken limbs and heals all wounds, while the second restores to life anyone who has thus been healed. Yet none can hope to descend the cleft or to bring back one drop of those waters, for the Rocks of Korsan are enchanted. Day and night they clash together, so that they crush and grind to pieces anything, however small, that may venture between them. Indeed, I never heard of any creature that even tried to do so.'

At this, every stork in the presence was silent, and at length the lord ordered that all in the court should assemble to hear the news of the king of Denmark's daughter. Still they had not a word to say, but only pecked at the ground and fanned their long, plumed tails, looking at one another sidelong.

At length, from the back of the crowd, there came limping up an old, tatter-feathered stork, lame in one foot and blind of an eye.

'May it please your lordship,' said he, 'I'll go for you and do the best I can. I'm not as young as I was, but at least I've learned a few tricks in my time and I've not got a fool's head on these old shoulders.'

The lord told the old stork that he was too frail and crippled to attempt a task by which even the youngest and strongest had good reason to feel daunted. Then he tried to persuade some of his captains to form a band to go together, but they all began to make excuses. At last – for he did not know what else to do – he said to the old stork, 'Do you really believe you can succeed?'

'Why, that I can't answer,' he replied, 'but just give me some grub for the journey and tie a bottle on each of these old pins of mine, and I promise your lordship that you won't see me again without they're full of that there water what you're after.'

The other birds began laughing at his rough talk and what they considered his conceit, but their lord, dismissing them angrily, took the old stork aside to prepare him for the adventure that no one else would attempt. He told him all he knew of the way – 'though after the Ice Isles,' said he, 'you'll just have to ask again of whom

you can, for no stork has travelled further' – tied the bottles to his legs and gave him as much food as he could carry. And then, at once, the old stork set out, while his lord sent a messenger to tell the king of Denmark that he had done all he could to help him and would send him further news as soon as might be.

The old stork flew on, over forest and river, forest, swamp and river, and then over the sea and over the ice. On he flew, until his old wings were tired out and he had but little food left. He asked the way of a shearwater, then of a storm petrel and then of a great albatross. The cold grew ever more bitter and the darkness longer, but at last, one desolate morning, he glimpsed in the distance, like two great towers, the Rocks of Korsan, which shook the near-by earth and sea as they continually clashed and clashed together with a sound that carried a hundred miles. All that morning he drew slowly nearer, until at last, as he still went on, he began to be buffeted and thrown about in the air by the continual turbulence as the enormous cliffs battered their opposing faces one against the other. Reaching them, he flew high above and, looking down into the dark, narrow cleft as it shut and opened, could see from moment to moment the faint glitter and sparkle of the miraculous springs gushing in the extreme depths.

Then, as he hesitated in fear and perplexity, there met him, in friendship, a bird – some say a swallow, but others say that it was the diver, with its blood-red throat, which called to him from the waves breaking on that desolate shore.

'Go no lower,' called the bird. 'Go no lower until noon, or thou art surely lost! Wait, wait and recover thy strength!'

'Alas, my friend,' replied the old stork, 'it's little enough strength I've got to recover, you know. Anyway, what good would it do me? They've sent me to fetch the waters of death and life, but it's plain enough there's no venturing down there; no, not for the strongest bird in the world, let alone an old tattercoat the likes of me.'

'Be advised,' said the other. 'Thou hast one chance. At noon each day the Rocks rest and sleep for half an hour. That will be soon. As soon as thou seest that a short time has passed and they do not move, then fly over the cleft and drop down into it as straight as a falling stone. Do not use thy wings. If the least pebble or flake of stone is dislodged, the Rocks will waken, close and kill thee.'

'But how do I get myself out again?' asked the old stork. 'I'll have to use my wings to mount, and besides, these bottles on my legs will be as heavy as two bricks.'

'That I cannot tell thee,' answered the bird. 'The lord does not exist for whom I would venture down to those waters: nor will I remain here longer, for the very noise and violence of the place fill me with fear.'

Not long after it had departed there fell a sudden quiet, in which the old stork could hear for the first time the splashing and trickling of the two springs in the heart of the abyss. Once more soaring over it, he looked down to judge his distance, then closed his wings and dropped.

As he entered the deep shadow between the Rocks and lost sight of the sun outside, he felt a terrible clutch of fear and almost opened his wings to fly out and escape. He had not realized how narrow the place would be. The jagged walls were so close on either side that he felt as though he were vanishing down a giant's throat – a cold throat, yet alive and ready at any moment to gulp and swallow him. He began to tremble in the dank, bitter cold and grew afraid that he would not be able to keep himself from blundering into one side or the other – the more so since he could scarcely see below him in the gloom. There was no sound but that of the water, which grew steadily louder as he descended.

At last he felt his legs touch ground, and here at least he was lucky, for he found himself on a rock midway between the two springs, so that he needed to take no more than a few steps to dip and fill first one bottle and then the other.

'This is no place to stop about,' thought he; and, peering up at the crack of light far above, he

opened his wings and began to fly.

He had not thought the bottles would be so heavy. He could not balance his old body against the hanging weight on his legs, but lurched backwards, flapping desperately as he tried to gain height. One of the cliffs seemed rushing towards him and just in time he swerved away, only to find the opposite face so close that his long bill passed between two projecting boulders. As he still rose higher he became all but exhausted, and so dizzy and confused that he almost alighted to rest on a ledge before realizing in the nick of time that this would mean his instant death. At every beat of his wings he felt the air driven back against his body from the sheer walls almost touching him on either side.

Suddenly, just below the top, he flew into the path of a sunbeam slanting down from above the southern side of the Rocks. Dazzled and taken by surprise, he closed his one eye against its brilliance, and in that moment blundered against the lip of the precipice. His feathers clattered in the silence and a pebble went plummeting and ringing down into the depths below.

Immediately he felt the Rocks move. The two cliffs were swaying, tilting, rushing forward, the push of air thrusting him upwards as the huge jaws, from base to summit, bit together along their entire length. His one thought was to save the water. As, desperately, he drew his legs up, his body once again tilted backwards and the Rocks, missing the bottles by inches, closed upon the long plumes of his tail, cutting through them like a shepherd's shears. Wrenching himself free, he looked down to see the Rocks grind open again and his tail feathers float down and out of sight into the shadows.

Breathless and shaking, the old stork turned out of the sun and gazed round at the sea and land below. There was no sign of the bird who had befriended him; and there was certainly nothing to remain for. Weighed down by the bottles and unbalanced by the loss of his tail, he set off on the return journey.

At last, worn out and half-starved – for he had eaten the last of his food three days before – he arrived back at the court of the stork lord. It was now assembly time and great crowds of storks were gathered from every quarter. For some time he could not find the lord, but at last he caught sight of him in the centre of a crowd of storks gathered together on the edge of the lake. It was never permitted to fly into the lord's presence, so he alighted in the shallow water a little way off. As he came stumbling his way ashore, with the heavy bottles on his legs, all the other storks began laughing and jeering at his ridiculous, ugly appearance and the crushed and broken stump of his tail. Then some of them began pushing and jostling him.

'Look at old Stumpy!' shouted one young stork. 'Doesn't he look smart? Come on, let's smash his silly bottles!'

At this the lord looked round, saw who it was that was coming and, in a tremendous voice that silenced everyone, cried out 'Stop!' Then, approaching and himself helping the old stork forward, he turned to those around them and said, 'When you have flown between the Rocks of Korsan yourselves, then, if you still want to, you may jeer at another who has. Meanwhile, you are not fit to wear plumes. From this time forth not one of you shall have a better tail than his.'

The whole assembly looked one at another and saw that it was even as their lord had said. Their tails had vanished, and from that day to this no stork has had anything but the stumpy tail we see today.

So the king's daughter was saved, but what reward they gave to the old stork I never heard. They say that – Look, isn't that Jarl down there in the lane now, just beyond the hawthorn bushes? Why don't you run down and see him? It needn't be bedtime just yet.

THE IRON WOLF

I dare say they won't be so very long changing horses, Your Excellency. And then you're off again to the North, I dare say?

Well, well, you needn't mind me asking questions. We're inclined to speak freely, us Caucasus folk, you know. More than your serfs up North, very like. Feel free, speak free, that's about the size of it. I've Cossack blood, you know – plenty of it – and there's plenty been spilled, time was.

I'm an old man, you'd say, wouldn't you? And I dare say that young landlord yonder – younger than my grandson, he must be – he's told you I'm a silly old fellow as would pitch you a tall story if you bought him a drink, eh? Oh, yes, I'm sure he did, Your Excellency, begging your pardon. These smart young town chaps today, they don't believe anything without it's all written down and signed, or else printed in one of these here newspapers. Doesn't matter, then, how many lies there are on the paper, they'll believe the lot. There's just two good uses I know for a newspaper, Your Excellency, and one of them's rolling up tobacco for smoking.

Well, now, that's exceedingly kind of you, sir. I'll be glad to sit down and have a bit of a smoke with you while you're waiting. Thirsty work, smoking, Your Honour, don't you agree? Come to that, waiting's apt to be thirsty work too. Very warm weather just now – very dry.

Ah, now, if only all gentlemen were like Your Excellency! Here's your very good health, sir! That's uncommonly good vodka! Polish, is it? I thought as it had a tang of herbs to it, like. You're wise to carry a bottle with you.

The Iron Wolf? Well, now, I dare say it was that young Sergei round in the stable as told you to ask me to tell you about the Iron Wolf? Oh,

I'll lay as it was. Well, I can tell you, sir, sure enough; but it's no matter for joking, and I'll tell you that, too. I suppose Sergei said old Ivan Stepanovich was good for a tall story to pass your time while you had to wait?

Your Excellency's very kind – very kind indeed. And you're quite right – grandchildren do take a deal of feeding and that. Well, sir, I'll tell you the tale – and it's true – but I'd just like to make so bold as to hope you won't go making a joke of it, nor nothing of that sort, when you're back among all your ladies and gentlemen in St Petersburg. They may well thank the holy St Michael, ay, and Frola and Lavra too, that *they* never saw the Iron Wolf. You just tell 'em that, now.

The good book says thou shalt not be afraid for any terror by night nor for the arrow that flieth by day, but it says nought of the Iron Wolf – and no great wonder at all, I should say, for that's a book that tells no lies and who wouldn't be afraid for a creature that's worse than the Nightmare and the three-headed dog of Hades put together? Now me, I'm a very lucky man, sir – always was. I've fought in two wars and lost three fingers from frostbite; I've made a decent enough fortune and seen it vanish like snow in the spring. I've stood and watched my fine timber house burn to the ground and the smoke go up to the sky, and once I nearly died of fever in the Caspian swamps. But I never saw the Iron Wolf, and that's the greatest luck in the world, for once I was near enough to him – ay, a great deal too near. This is the way it was.

There was a fine young fellow as I knew, name of Peter, strong as a bear and almost as steady as a winter evening's rain; and you know how steady that can be, I dare say, and you a traveller yourself. Well, he was reliable enough, except maybe when he got to feeling pleased with himself and anyone bought him an extra drink or two, and then he might start jumping over a barn roof or pushing down a haystack, just to pass an hour or two till morning. But at the time I'm speaking of, he wasn't getting up to any of those tricks, for he was working for an old priest down Stavropol way, and giving very good service too, for he could do as much as three men when he gave himself to it, and that was often enough, for he liked the old fellow, who left him pretty much to himself – trusted him, you know, to see what wanted doing and then get on with it – and quite often used to come down almost as handsome as Your Honour, with a new pair of shoes or half a bottle of vodka that was no part of their contract at all – a bit extra, as the old woman said when she left the washing out all night and the starlings roosted on the clothes line.

Well, one day, after six or seven years of this service, young Peter, he gets to thinking, 'If I don't move on a bit now and get out into the world I'll never make my fortune at all and I'll be stuck with dear old Father Gregory till the end of my days, for soon he'll have got the way he can't do without me, and I'll be too sorry for him to have the face to leave.' So off he goes to the back door, kisses the servant girl, eats two apples, drinks a glass of tea and nibbles three lumps of sugar in the kitchen and then has himself shown up to the old fellow in his study. He was very respectful, said all he should, and never told his business till the priest asked him straight out what it might be.

'Well, it's a long time now that I've been working for you, father,' he says, 'and if I've not displeased you I'd be glad to take what's coming to me and move on a bit. That's if you've no objection. I've a mind to set up for myself, you see.'

'Well, Peter,' says Father Gregory, 'I'm not saying I'll not be sorry, for you're a good lad and I'll miss you, that I shall. But you're a free man and entitled to better yourself if you can. The trouble is, you see, money's so tight just now that I can't lay my hands on the lump sum I'd like to pay you off. But don't go taking on now,' (for I dare say he saw the lad's face fall) 'I'll give you something I've got by me and that's this egg. You won't regret it, I'll tell you. It's no ordinary egg, that's for sure: and I never yet told you a lie nor cheated you, now did I? Wherever it is you're going to, take the egg with you; and when you get there and not before, make yourself a good, strong cattle-pen and break the egg in the middle of it. Then you'll see something that couldn't be beat by forty-five prophets, two judges and a saint – no, nor yet by our little father the Tsar and all his generals. But whatever you do, my boy, don't break the egg till you've made the preparations, or all your luck will be gone as fast as gypsies the morning after the hens have vanished.'

Well, Peter had always trusted the old chap, and truth to tell he was a bit afraid of him too, for you never know, now do you, what power a priest may have? Anyway, the long and short of it was that he accepted the egg – and a queer, big sort of a roll-about thing it was, with a shine on it like a wet wall in the moonlight – thanked his master kindly and off he goes, striding along like a good'un and feeling pretty cheerful to think he was out of service and free to make his own way in the world. He got a lift in a cart and a bit later he got another in a carriage – oh yes, a real nobleman's carriage – for it was empty, d'ye see, and the coachman, who was only out exercising the horses, said to be sure he might just as well use Peter as ballast and take him a bit on his way, seeing as the master was nowhere near to find fault. Then he stopped at an inn for a meal and a few nips of vodka and off he went again, out on to the steppe and no more than five versts to go to see the smoke from his old mother's chimney – not that it's different from any other smoke, you know, but you try telling that to a fellow that hasn't seen it in a long while.

Now the egg was all wrapped up for safety and he'd even sewn down the flap of his coat over it, but just the same he felt as though it were burning a hole in his pocket. He trusted in that egg, you see, to hold something truly marvellous, and that was because he trusted old Father Gregory. But what in the name of fortune could be in it, he kept wondering. 'A strong pen' the

priest had said he had to build – but how could that square with whatever could be inside an egg? Well, one thought led to another and he couldn't keep track of them, like looking out of the window on a winter's afternoon to watch the snowflakes falling (you mustn't forget those nips of vodka), and what happened – oh dear, oh dear – was that in the end he just lost patience altogether; and he put down the egg on the bare steppe – not a soul in sight – and knocked it open very clean, cracking it in two with a tap of his knife.

Oh, holy saints! Have you ever stood and watched wasps coming out of their hole in the bank? Or sparks out of the back of the chimney? Or dust when a carpet's beaten? It was like the gushing of a spring and altogether worse than some stupid old fellow telling a tale that can't stop talking. (You needn't look at me, sir.) For it was *cattle* that came out of the egg – ay, cattle – black and white and brown and shaggy and smooth and long-horned and short, all the breeds there are and a good many there aren't, like the Toreador's Knockout and the Bashan Blue. The whole steppe became like a fair, and all mooing and champing at the grass and flop-flopping and trampling up the ground. Poor Peter stood there as fairly out of his depth as a mouse at a mass and 'Saints and angels!' says he to himself, 'whatever am I going to do now? What a fool I've been, to have gone and wasted, ay, poured away a gift that would have made me the richest man from Krasnodar to Astrakhan!' He was ready to cry, and all the while the great beasts jostling round him and pushing and rolling their eyes and slavering over his boots, and him with not even a stick in his hand. They were rambling away, too, the outer ones were, heading for the horizon and nothing to stop them at all.

And then, all of a sudden, there was another beast standing before him – a beast the cattle couldn't see, or so you'd have thought – but Peter could see it all right; and as he looked, the green meadows of his heart turned to cinders

within him, for he knew he was face to face with the Iron Wolf. For that's how the Iron Wolf comes, you know, sir – just when you're altogether desperate and can't tell whether you're dreaming or waking or whatever you're going to do at all. Some say he's never very far off, but that those who see him can do so only at such a time as that. I never heard but the one man that tried to say what he was like. 'He's made all of a thick, dark smoke,' he said. 'You'd think it was off the bonfire that burns the damned, and nothing alight in it but just the eyes.'

Young Peter looks at the Iron Wolf and the Iron Wolf looks at Peter from those eyes, that had no pupils to them. What he said came to Peter all right, but not through his ears. That was like a smoke too – like a fume in his head.

'You're in a sad case, young Peter – like to lose your fortune, eh?' says the Iron Wolf.

Peter just nodded, for he couldn't speak.

The Iron Wolf seemed to lick his lips and look about him for a while among the cattle. At last he said, 'Well, I'll collect your cattle, if you like, and drive them back into the egg again; ay, and patch it up just as good as new. That sort of thing's quite up my street, you know – it's the kind of work that's been put in my power to do.' And at this he grinned just as amiably as a madman drowning a cat in a tub.

Never a word said Peter, but only dropped his eyes towards the two halves of the egg lying on the ground at his feet.

'Well, it's a bargain between us then,' says the Iron Wolf. 'I'll oblige you in this little matter, and in return, whenever you may come to sit down on the bridal bench, I'll just come round and gobble you up.'

'The bridal bench?' thought Peter, as well as he could think at all. 'Well, that's no part of my plans just now, but at this rate the cattle will all be out of sight in twenty minutes. What can I do? I've been a fool once – if I get out of this fix I'll never be such a fool again.'

'Agreed!' he shouted – and that was the only word he ever spoke in all his life to the Iron Wolf, for with that the Wolf leaps into the air like a great, writhing snake and turns himself into six hundred and sixty-six sheep-dogs, all barking and driving together round the herd. The shadow of a blade of grass wouldn't have moved across a daisy before all those thousands of cattle were back in the egg and the egg was mended as whole as the reflections in a pond when the ripples have settled. But when young Peter looked round for the Iron Wolf he was nowhere to be seen. There's a good many cracks in the ground, you know, and if they're narrow that's little enough hindrance to the kind of creature for whom they're the quickest way home.

Peter picked up the egg, and very sober he found himself all of a sudden; and he went the rest of the way to his village as if he was coming home from church. In fact his old mother, when she'd done hugging and kissing him and cooking him the finest supper she could lay her hands on – when she was sitting by the fire before bedtime, in fact – found herself thinking that service with the priest seemed to have steadied him up a good deal – even turned him from a youth into a man. He should be equal to most things likely to come along, she thought, for he had the air of a fellow that had been through some very deep water.

Well, the second time he broke the egg, you can be sure he took good care to do it the right way, in the middle of the strongest pen he could build, and six or seven more beyond that again, to take the overflow. What the neighbours thought I never heard tell. For all I know they may have put it down to witchcraft. But after all, the cattle were there to be seen, and you don't go finding fault or calling names – now do you? – with a fellow that's the richest man for miles around and never done you any harm, very free with his hospitality and ready enough to relieve the poor or give a man a job. Young Peter took to farming and cattle-breeding and it all turned out very well, for he worked and didn't spare himself from morning to night. Even with the certain makings of a fortune you've still got to work to get it, as I dare say you know well enough, sir. Ay, it's a hard world for sure, as the schoolmaster's cat said when the globe fell on his head.

There was one thing in the back of his mind, like a stone in his boot or a shred of meat between his teeth, for he couldn't be rid of it. 'Twas the Iron Wolf, of course. He'd have liked to marry. He was the age to marry and everyone was wondering why he didn't, not least his old mother. She didn't nag him about it – not at all – she was a decent old soul and treated him as the head of the family, which he was. But he could tell what she was thinking as sure as he could tell when rain was coming or when a girl had taken a fancy to him – you don't need words, let alone that foolish writing, for a great many matters, and not the least important things in life either. Of course there was any number of girls dreamed of him and woke up in a cold bed, as the saying goes. There wasn't a better catch in the country round, and one way and another he was a bit of a mystery to the local gossips, for he could have taken his pick.

Now not far away there lived an old General – a widower and a very distinguished man, with a big estate and a great reputation. They did say as he'd fought and beaten just about every enemy from Genghis Khan to Napoleon, but if he had, it was little enough he'd got out of it, for he hadn't enough to keep up his estate, you know, and if the barn roofs wanted repair it was because there was no money to paint the back stairs, for it had been spent on filling up the duck-pond after the ducks had been sold. You know how it is. A good general can give all he has and the states-men just send him home at the end, for he's no more good to them then. No, not once the war's done and ended. Harvest's in and hands can go.

But there was one fine jewel the General had, and that was his daughter, Marienka. She hadn't been more than a lass at school when Peter came home, but by the time she was eighteen she was just the most beautiful girl you could well find in a week's march, a month's journey and a year in Moscow. Peter met her up at the hall more than

once, for the truth was he used to help the old General out a bit, lending him money and so on and never in much of a hurry to see it back, either: and that was just as well, for the money was no more going to return to him than those clouds out there. It rains into the sea, you know, but the sea's still salt for all that.

Marienka knew how to make her feelings for Peter clear enough and he'd have had to be made of leather not to feel his heart turn over. She was a fine lady, you understand, and might have been entitled to call herself Countess or Princess or something of that sort. But of course a title's no more use without money than a boat without a sail – you may stay afloat but you won't go far.

Anyway, young Peter got the way he was fairly wild for love of Marienka and could no more help himself than a swarm of bees in June. And the old General saw how it was and put his silence down to bashfulness and respect for the quality, which he thought very proper and flattering in a young farmer, even one as rich as Peter. But when he thought of his barn roofs mended and himself back in the drawing-rooms of the capital, with all his decorations on and a carriage at the door to take him home drunk or sober, he thought he'd just set to and bring it about himself. So one evening he spoke very civil to Peter and pulled the conversation round that way. What with his longing for Marienka, it fairly broke the poor lad down and he ended by telling the General all about the egg and the Iron Wolf and the bargain he'd made.

'Don't you worry yourself about that, my dear boy,' says the old General, stroking his moustache as he helped himself to another glass of wine and passed Peter the bottle. 'I'll just write to the Colonel of my old regiment and ask him for a guard of honour for the occasion – three hundred of 'em, if you like, with muskets and bayonets. I don't suppose the Iron Wolf was at Borodino, no, nor yet at Sebastopol neither. If he turns up here he's in for a shock.'

Peter cast his mind back to that evening on the steppe and somehow there was a doubt in his happy mind, hard as the stone inside a cherry, whether the Iron Wolf was likely to find the General's men much of a let or hindrance in running any race he'd set before him. But you know how it is with a man in love – he thought of it a bit and he'd got no answer, so he let it go and thought about Marienka instead. Certainly she was much easier to think about than the Iron Wolf.

Well, the wedding day came and so did all the people for miles around, and the guard of honour too, in their regimentals and polished boots. The old General had put on a spread fit to bust the tables and old Father Gregory himself travelled over to lend a hand with the service. The weather was beautiful – early September and everyone delighted with a good harvest – and the band was playing on the terrace when the time came for the two young people to be cheered all the way and then to sit down together on the bridal bench.

The old General had his men round the house – three lines of them, all soldiers fit to storm Constantinople. And just as the people were throwing roses and the corks were popping like a stockman's whip, up comes the Iron Wolf out of the wood beyond the bowling-green. Those that didn't see him were the lucky ones – they followed those that did and they ran just as fast. Fear's like fire, after all. You may know what started it and then again you may not, but it'll burn your house down just the same. For all the fighting they did, the three lines of soldiers might have been scarecrows, snowmen and waxworks, and I don't remember to have heard anyone that blamed them, either.

Peter had just time to grab Marienka by the arm and over the wall they went and straight into the stable-yard. The General had a horse called Rocket and he was still saddled and hitched to the trough, for as it happened the General had had a fancy to ride him to church that day – no doubt so that everyone could get a good look at his medals and his uniform. Peter slung the girl across the saddle, all in her bridal dress, and out

of the yard they went like a shooting star. They galloped faster than cloud-shadows on the steppe and after them came the Iron Wolf. The horse knew what was behind him all right, for he went quicker than ever he'd gone before, and that's saying more than a little.

Well, they lost the Iron Wolf all right – put him behind them before evening. But that was small enough comfort, and myself I've always believed he was playing with them; for where could they turn now and what was the young fellow to do? Those that can mend a broken egg can smash a lock, I dare say, and those that can disappear down a crack in the ground can find a runaway wherever he may have got to. At nightfall Peter and Marienka found themselves in a thick forest and the horse so spent that Peter dismounted and led it down the rides.

They came to a hut and he knocked on the door. An old couple let them in, staring at the bridal clothes all covered in mud, the dead-beat horse and the young man that kept peering behind him into the dusk. After a little the old man said, 'I suppose your father-in-law's not far behind, young fellow, with a pistol or two in his belt – is that the way of it?'

'Would to God it were!' says Peter. 'It's not my father-in-law that's behind me; it's the Iron Wolf himself.'

'Chutko! Chutko!' calls the old fellow, and up jumps a great, bristling hound from behind the stove, with the look of a creature that ate three dragons every morning before breakfast. 'You lie down and sleep, now,' says the old man. 'Chutko'll tell us if the Iron Wolf's coming, no danger.'

Peter looked at Chutko and the more he looked at him the more he thought as that would be the dog to have beside you in a tight place.

'Will you sell him?' says he to the old chap. 'I'll pay you very well indeed.' For he thought, do you see, that he might set Chutko on to fight the Iron Wolf and even drive him away. The old chap scratched his head and said he didn't know about that, but he knew all right when Peter offered him a sum that would have bought a bull and a boar and a shed to keep them in. He took the money, gave the young people their supper and showed them where to sleep.

It was early morning when Chutko began to bark like a foundry hammer and up jumps Peter and opens the door. Chutko dashed out, but he stopped barking when he caught sight of the Iron Wolf coming through the trees. However, he was still a long way off and by the time Peter and Marienka had mounted Rocket and caught up with Chutko he was further off still, for the dog went faster than the horse if anything, and all round them the birds flying up in the silence. Oh yes, Chutko was a good dog right enough, but he was as much afraid of the Iron Wolf as any Christian man.

They went on and on and they came to the mountains – ay, the Bolshoi Kavkaz, the cloud cutters: you've seen them, sir, no doubt, and Mount Elbrus, where the Wicked One took Our Lord, they say, and showed Him all the kingdoms of the world in a moment of time. Well, 'twas somewhere on the western end of the range and high above the sea that they happened on a lonely castle, hanging half-way down the forest slopes like a chip in a woodcutter's beard. They roused none but the gatekeeper, and him they begged for shelter: only this time young Peter and Marienka slept by the horse, with everything prepared for flight in a moment. For truth to tell, he'd become desperate, you see. He didn't believe he could escape the Iron Wolf and he had no plan in mind but only to run and to keep on

running. All the same, he bought a second dog from the gatekeeper – a beast called Vazhko, that looked half like a wolf itself and would hold its grip with a live coal burning an inch from its nose. It wasn't that he had any hope, but he meant to sell his life as dear as he could; and he thought, too, that the Iron Wolf might likely finish with him in some lonely place at last and then the dogs – or what was left of them – might be some protection to Marienka after he'd been taken away to – well, to wherever he was taken away to.

It was a bad outlook; and it was worse still at midnight, when the dogs began to bark. Yes, at midnight, or soon after, for the Iron Wolf hadn't taken so long now to find them out and catch up with them. Out into the dark they went and left the way to Rocket and the two dogs, and they went fast enough, for they could smell the Iron Wolf behind them. Later there was a bit of a moon, but Peter had as lief there hadn't been, for the ways they came by would have put the fear of God into a mountain goat and he'd no wish to see them.

When they came to the sea the dawn was breaking and the rain was coming down like broom-handles. That's when *my* dog began to bark, and I looked out of my hut and saw them coming, for I was working as a fisherman at that time, a fair way out from Sakhumi. I like a lonely place for that kind of work, where you're not fishing in other fellows' pockets all day long. My boat was beached, as luck would have it, for I'd sprung two planks the day before and hauled her out for repair.

The young man came up; and I stared, I can tell you, to see the spent horse and the limping dogs, the lovely girl in a wedding dress all to flinders and the young man with a look on him like a cat at the top of a tree on fire.

'Will you sell me your boat?' says he, and when I answered it wasn't sound he gives a kind of groan and turns round to the girl.

'There's no going on from here, my darling,' says he. 'Forgive me the wrong I've done you,

and think as well of me as you can, for I loved you true enough, indeed I did. Then sell me that dog,' says he to me. 'Here's a purse of gold for him – enough and more, no bargains – and now, take my Marienka into the hut with you and don't let her come out, whatever there is to be heard.'

I did as he told me very sharp and so would you have, sir, I've a notion. It had got as dark as a crypt and the waves beating the shore like an archangel's wings on Judgement Day. I gave him Bary, that was a good dog – best I ever had – and took the girl indoors. I thought she'd cry, but she didn't. No, she just stood up straight by the table and said never a word, only she was listening, you know, and her face and her knuckles very white.

Then the Iron Wolf came down out of the mountains, and of that I can tell you nothing at all, for I was under the bed and praying to God and Saint Basil, and felt as though I was falling through a sky with no bottom and neither up nor down. Once I opened my eyes. If the sun had a ghost in another world, sir, that would be the light it would shed, and by that light I saw the girl standing at the window.

'Will you come away?' I whispered, and I dare say I must have sounded like a dying man begging for water. She didn't answer.

'The dogs,' she said, as if she were talking to herself. 'The dogs won't leave him. They'll die for him first.'

Then I heard a thump on the boards and I knew the lad had set his back to the shed outside. There was a few moments' silence – no growling, no yelping – and then a voice, very low; and all I can tell you is that that voice was speaking a tongue as was foreign to it. It was as though some great insect might have learned human speech, and that's all I want to say about it.

'Your dogs have wounded me. I'll kill you, Peter, but the matter won't be ended there.'

And then I heard the door open and shut and when I looked again the girl was gone. The lad shouted 'Marienka!' and then she says, very clear and level, 'You'll kill me first,' she says. 'Do you think I don't love him better than the dogs?'

And with that there came a howl as though you'd snatched the prey from forty famished tigers. Oh ay, you think I'm a coward, no doubt – but if you'd heard it, you'd have fainted as I did. Yes, I fainted clean away, and when I came to, the girl was bathing my head with sea-water and the lad was tending the dogs, that was lying bleeding on the floor. They put me in my own bed, but it came on sunny and warm by mid-day and I was quite myself again, and even got to mending the boat before sunset.

Peter? He's up Georgiyevsk way now, and Marienka too – three or four fine sons growing up, and old Bary remembered me all right the last time I was there, wagging his tail. Ah, he's a plucky dog, that one. Well, I won't say no to another nip, sir, since you're so pressing, and thank you kindly. But if I do, I shan't be able to tell you any more tales, and a good job too, I dare say you're thinking. Here's your very good health, sir, and may the saints shoe your horse and light your lantern before you for ever! There's young Sergei bringing your carriage round now. What did Your Excellency say your name might be? Count Leo Tolstoy? Well, if the crows don't snatch it away out of my head, I'll remember it as long as I've got five wits, two eyes and one throat. God bless you, sir!

THE NIGHTINGALE

Perhaps you'd better come out now, darling. The water's still a bit cold, don't you think? Later on, in July, you'll be able to stay in as long as you like.

No, we needn't go home yet if you don't want to. Daddy won't be back until at least half past six. He's got to stop on the way to see a man in Pangbourne. No, of course he won't have forgotten the transfers. If there are any transfers between here and Reading, Daddy will have got them, you can be sure of that.

Isn't it quiet? Look – see the water-rat, over on the other bank? No, running along there, just the other side of that clump of meadow-sweet. There he goes, plop! Well, he saw you drying your hair. He knows there's nothing natural round here as bright as that towel.

Oh, listen, there's a nightingale! Can you hear him? Wait a moment! Yes, there he is again; not very far away, either – somewhere down in those holly bushes. They don't sing only by night, you know; they sing a lot in the day-time too, but they nearly always keep themselves hidden in thick bushes. Yes, of course you can go and have a look for him if you like, but you won't see him. Yes, I'll come.

We're being teased, aren't we? Wherever you look, he starts singing somewhere else. Let's go back to the bank and lie in the sun.

You hardly ever do see them, actually, and anyway they're not much to look at – the dullest little brown bird you can imagine, about as big as a sparrow. They don't always sing as beautifully as that, either. Sometimes they just go on saying 'Chuk, chuk, chuk' for an hour on end. We're lucky to have heard him in full song.

Look out, that's a horsefly! Smack it! Well done – that's the end of him! What was I going to say? Oh, yes, there's a story about how the nightingale got his voice. I'll see if I can remember it, if you like. Miss Langdon used to tell it to us. That's a long time ago – longer than I care to remember.

They say that once upon a time, soon after the beginning of the world, all the birds were much the same to look at, except for their different sizes. They were all just sort of brown on top and greyish-white or stone colour underneath, and they all had the same kind of beaks; ordinary, short, straight ones.

Well, one day God was walking round the world, looking at all the wonderful things he'd made, and suddenly it occurred to him that the birds were rather dull and that he could improve them and make them something special. So he told Gabriel to get everything ready and then summon all the birds to assemble on a particular day, because he was going to make them look different and really splendid.

When the day came, there were crowds of

birds gathered – all the birds in the world. The meeting-place was a big, green hill, and Gabriel had quite a job getting them all to keep quiet while he counted them and ticked them off on his list to make sure none was missing. And then the magpie stole the list for a joke and when Gabriel got it back again it was a bit scratched and muddy. Anyway, finally he decided that everyone must have arrived (he'd made a mistake, as you'll see) and he told God they were ready to start.

God arrived with a huge bag, full of different beaks, and carrying his paint-box. The colours in the box were self-perpetuating and everlasting, and they were so wonderful and extraordinary that even God wouldn't be able to make any more. He asked the jay politely to be quiet and then explained to all the birds that he'd decided it would be a marvellous idea to paint them, and that each of them would be allowed to choose his own colours and his own beak. The birds cheered and got very excited and then they all sat down or flew about, waiting for their turns and talking to each other about the different colours they were going to have.

The first bird to come up was the macaw and he fairly did himself proud. No one's ever seen anything like it from that day to this. D'you remember him in the zoo? God and Gabriel were careful not to laugh, but they couldn't help just catching each other's eyes as the macaw kept on asking for a bit more of the red and then a bit more of that very bright blue in the corner. When they'd finished, he chose a big, strong, hooked beak that he could crack nuts with, and back he flew to Africa, as pleased as Punch and fairly squawking with pride.

The blackbird came up next, although he hadn't got that name yet. He'd been watching while they painted the macaw and he'd seen the other birds laughing behind their wings. So he chose a beautiful, plain, glossy black, and then he cocked his tail and looked all round and went 'T'ck, t'ck, t'ck,' as much as to say 'Now then, who's going to laugh at that?' All the same, he couldn't resist a bright-yellow beak he saw in the bag, and everyone said it set off the black very well. Before he left he flew up into a beech tree and sang a beautiful song of thanks.

One by one, all the birds came up in their turns and chose their colours. The thrush sat up very straight and still while his breast was dotted with brown spots, and you can just imagine what a lot of trouble the peacock gave before he was satisfied. He couldn't even sing about it either, but God didn't mind. He just went on painting,

for he loved all his birds – whinchats and blackcaps, yellow wagtails, waxwings and red-throated swallows. There was one enormous beak that God thought he'd made wrong and he was going to throw it away, but the pelican said, 'Just a moment, Lord, I believe it would suit me very well:' and so it did, for he's kept it ever since.

It was a beautiful summer day – just like this one – and even the humming-birds didn't feel cold. At last, as evening was falling, God saw that there were only a few birds remaining, and he told them that they could go ahead and use up all the paint he had left, because he'd mixed it that morning specially and it wouldn't keep. So the kingfisher and the bee-eater and the green woodpecker and the hoopoe and the oriole and one or two more took him at his word, and had themselves fairly covered with marvellous blues and greens and pinks and yellows.

At last every single bird had come and gone, and there were no beaks left and all the wonderful paint was gone too; and God washed his hands in the brook – What? Well, I don't see why not. It says 'sitteth at the right hand of God' doesn't it? – and he and Gabriel went strolling away down the hill together, feeling pretty tired, I dare say, but very much pleased with their long day's work.

'That's improved the world no end, Lord,' said Gabriel, as they came to the wood at the foot of the hill. 'Just look at that chaffinch sitting on the elder there, with his slate-blue top-knot.'

The chaffinch sang, 'Will you, will you, will you, will you *kiss* me, dear?' and God laughed as he flew away in the twilight, flashing the white feathers along his wings.

Just at that moment they both heard a fluttering and a kind of commotion down in the wood. Something was coming along through the bushes, and evidently in a great hurry too, for the leaves were rustling and twigs were snapping, and yet there was nothing to be seen. They both waited to find out what it could be, but it was nearly dark now and they couldn't make out very much at all.

God was just turning away, when suddenly a little grey-and-brown bird flew out of the haw-thorn, piping 'Lord! Lord!' It was the nightingale. God stretched out his arm and the nightingale perched on his wrist.

'They told me – told me – the blackbird told me just now that you'd asked – you'd asked everybody to come and be painted,' gasped the nightingale. 'He said I ought to have heard about it before, but I live in the thick bushes down in the wood and nobody remembered to come and tell me. I hurried here as soon as I heard. I'm not too late, Lord, am I?'

God looked into the wonderful paint-box. It was absolutely bare. Every single colour was gone, all used up. The little bird looked too, and when he saw the box was empty he couldn't control a sob of bitter disappointment. He felt it was all his own fault, and he was just going to fly away when God noticed the brushes, lying in their place at one side of the box. On the tip of one of them was left a glittering speck of gold.

'Just sit here on my finger a moment,' said God, 'and open your beak.'

The little brown bird did as he was told, and God took the brush and gently touched his tongue with the speck of gold. It tasted sharp and burning and he flew away quickly into the bushes. Then, suddenly, he began to sing. No one in all the world had ever heard any bird sing like that. The farmer, driving his cows home to milking, stopped in amazement. The shepherd on the hill forgot his sheep and stood staring into the dusk, and his wife, who was tucking their little boy up in bed, came to the window and listened as though an angel were singing.

God and Gabriel listened too, for a long time, and then they went home. They didn't need to ask the nightingale whether he was happy. It was a quiet night and they could still hear him half a mile away.

There's your nightingale again, now – he's gone further back into the wood. They never like anyone coming too close. Shall we go home? Daddy won't be long now.

How Long Will You Live?

Taff! Here, Taff, you can't go to muckin' sleep now, mate! Come on, Taffy, get a grip! It's time for stand-to! You remember what old Major Lonsdale said – we got to be fully alert at dusk and dawn. If the Jerries come over, that's when they'll be comin', mate, and I'm damned if they're goin' to get me without I get a few of them first. Ay, one for Jock and one for Corporal Metcalfe; and two for Captain Queripel an' all. Ought to get the bloomin' posthumous V.C., he ought. Taffy, listen! We *got* to keep awake this next half-hour, get it? I'll stick this bayonet in yer backside if you like, but you're not goin' to cop yer lot by droppin' off in this 'ere slit-trench.

How many grenades yer got left – two? That's two better than me, any road. Thank God we've got some Sten magazines! Yeah, an' poor old Jock's rifle and some of his 303. What's that yer got there, couple o' Jerry bakelites? Good luck to yer! I'm split-scared as five ruddy scalded cats, mate, an' I don't care who knows it. I was all right when we jumped. Ringway despatcher says, 'You're all right, ain't yer?' I says, 'Never better.' 'Can't even remember which day it was now, can you? I reckon I was O.K. right up until old Jock copped it. I was goin' off down the dressin' station with me wrist that night, I'll tell yer, an' I'd ha' bloomin' well stayed there an' all. On'y on the way I run into old Dickie Lonsdale, see? 'Where you goin', boy?' he says. 'You don't want to go down that so-and-so dressin' station,' he says. 'I'm countin' on you for another fourteen Jerries, Weston. Crackshot Weston, worth any other five.' 'Course it's all bull, he knows it and so do I, but what can yer say, an' 'im covered with blood and somethin' like forty field dressings. He takes out his flask. 'Take a swig of this, boy,' he says. 'That'll put yer right.' I says, 'When's the Second Army comin', sir?' 'When we've shot all the Jerries between ruddy Arnhem and Nijmegen,' he says. 'They might find enough guts to come then, so let's just get on with it, shall we?' He's a right lad, he is! One thing about bein' Airborne, 'least we got some officers – what's left of 'em.

When *is* the Second Army comin', that's what I want to know? Seven days, Taff, in't it, now? Was supposed to be two! Taff, for Christ's sake *wake up*! Here, listen, I know what! I'll tell yer a story, 's if yer were a kid, just to keep y' wake. Come on, now, listen! An' when I've done y' can tell it me back an' all, to show you *were* listenin'. All right? I'll tell yer one th' old parson used to tell us when I was a kid in Sunday school, an' by God do I wish I was back there? I'd give me lot, right now!

Well, at the beginnin' of the world, like, God was creatin' all the animals an' birds, an' decidin' what each one was goin' to have to do, sort of thing, an' how long it was going to have as a

natural life-span, see? And first of all he gets hold of the donkey, and he says to him, 'Now, how long do you want to live?' he says. 'How about thirty years? Will that do you all right?'

'Well,' says the donkey, 'I dunno as I'm so very keen,' he says. Yer listenin', Taff, are yer? 'I dunno as I'm so very keen. I'm just going to have to carry a lot of heavy loads about all day and half the bloomin' night, and get beaten for my trouble an' worked till I drop,' he says. 'Can't you make it a bit less? I reckon it's best over soon.'

So God says, 'All right, I'll knock off eighteen years and you can have twelve.' 'Thanks very much,' says the donkey, an' off he goes.

Any road, next of all up comes the camel, and God says, 'Well, you're tough enough,' he says.

'I'm going to give you thirty years to enjoy yourself in the desert.'

'I don't want all that,' says the camel. 'Just hard work in the boilin' hot sun and whoever gets any good of it, I shan't.'

So God promised to reduce his life to twenty years.

Well, then the dog's up at the head of the queue; and God says to him, 'And how long do *you* want to live? I suppose you'll be happy enough with – well, let's say twenty-seven years, shall we?'

'Will we hell as like!' says the dog. 'Runnin' about, chasin' sheep here, there and everywhere, drivin' beasts to market with yer throat full of dust, workin' yer pads sore, and lucky if you get enough to eat from some old farmer who just puts you down when you've got too old! Can't you cut it down?' he says to God. So God said, 'Well, all right then,' he says, 'I'll take away twelve years, and give you fifteen.'

Well, by this time God was beginnin' to think that the animals weren't really respondin' very

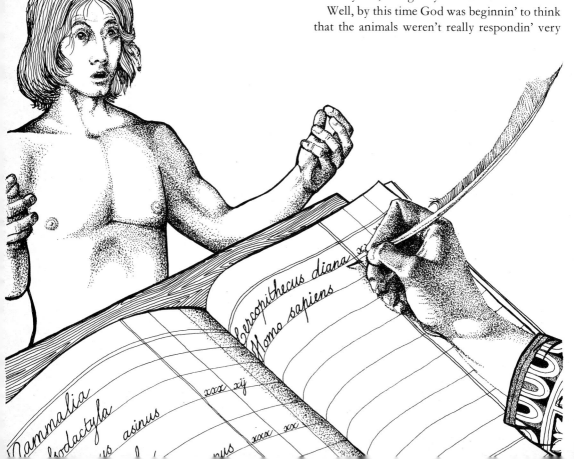

well to all his great ideas as he'd thought they were goin' to be so pleased with, so he called the next animal out hisself and it was the monkey.

'Now look,' he says, 'the others didn't fancy a nice long life, on account of the work, but you're different. You aren't going to have to work. So I'll just give you thirty years instead of them. What about it?'

'Well, I wish you wouldn't,' answered the monkey. 'It ain't my fancy at all. I know I always look very happy, playin' tricks and grabbin' things and swingin' about an' that, but it ain't really all that much fun, what with the insects, and the trouble of gettin' enough to eat, and then there's all the snakes an' that, what we can't avoid – we're always afraid. I'd say twenty years would be quite enough, myself. Too much, if anything.'

So God makes it twenty years for the old monkey.

And then he thought to hisself, 'Well, this can't go on. *Someone's* got to appreciate this gift of life that I've got to give away. I'll have to make a special animal, like, that's really goin' to go for it in a big way.' So he created Man.

'Now,' he says to the man, 'here we bloomin' well go at last. *You'll* live thirty years, won't you?'

'Good grief!' says the man, 'that ain't nothin' like long enough! That the best you can do?'

'Well,' says God, 'I reckoned it was handsome, myself. Still, anything to oblige,' he says. 'Tell you what! I've got a buckshee eighteen years what I took off the donkey at his own request. You can have those.'

'But that's not enough!' says the man. 'Come on, surely you got some more somewhere, ain't yer?'

'Well, all right,' says God, 'since you're so appreciative, you can have the twelve years what I took off the dog an' all.'

'I call that mingey,' says the man. 'I've a good

mind to go on strike,' he says. 'What yer got in that there sack? I bet yer got some more salted away, y' old beggar! What's the good of just sixty years to a bloke like me?'

'I *have* got some more,' says God. 'I got ten years from the camel's little bit an' ten years what the monkey don't want. You can have them, mate, an' I hope it keeps fine for yer an' all. An' if that's not enough, yer can just go an' jump in the flippin' lake, 'cos there ain't no more between 'ere an' Jericho,' he says.

So that was the end of the man's little lot. And ever since then he lives thirty years what's his own, like, when he enjoys hisself properly and lives it up. And then he does the donkey's eighteen, when he has to work harder and harder and has more and more to worry about. And if he gets through that lot, he can do ten years for the camel, with a bad temper an' livin' off of hisself, like, an' keepin' on about things ain't what they used to be when he was young. After that he has another twelve for the old dog, lyin' in a corner and growlin' and eatin' what he can with three old teeth in his head. And if that's not enough for him, then he can just finish off with ten for the monkey, daft in the nut and doin' silly things like a little kid, until he snuffs it. So cheer up, Taff! Yer goin' ter be all right!

Here, it's daylight, mate, ain't it? Reckon we could stand down, don't you? Them damned Jerry mortars'll be startin' up again any minute now. We'd best get down inside.

'Ere, who's this comin'? Cor, it's Major Dickie ruddy Lonsdale! Here, sir, over here, quick, in 'ere, sir!

Oh, thank you very much, sir. Williams an' me's been clean out of fags since last night. Just the job, this is. Got a light, sir? Thanks. Any news? When's the Second Army comin', sir? They're *bound* to get to Arnhem today, aren't they?

═BACK OF THE MOON═

Hullo, Julie; can't you sleep? Are you too hot? Why not chuck off the eiderdown? And that top blanket, I would. I don't know why it is, but nine times out of ten, if you have what I used to call 'frightening thoughts' in bed, it's because you're too hot. 'Seems to induce them, for some reason.

Oh, the moon, is it? Too bright? Did you know that people used to say that sleeping with the moon shining on your face made you mad? That's why mad people were called 'lunatics'. But it doesn't, so don't worry.

Let's have a look out of the window for a bit. Can you smell the night-scented stock? It *is* bright moonlight, isn't it? Almost like day. 'Vega conspicuous overhead, in the windless nights of June.' And that's Jupiter, that very bright one. 'So bright as almost to cast a shadow', as Thomas Hardy said. And the red one, low down – that's Antares. It only looks red because it's in the horizon haze. If we were in Tahiti, it would be up in the zenith, and bright silver.

Cock pheasant! Hear him, somewhere up by the beeches along the top? And there's Mr Jackson, look, out at his pheasant coops. He *is* a good gamekeeper. It's all round the clock with him. If I were Lord Iliffe, I'd value Mr Jackson very highly. He hardly needs that torch, does he, with the moon so bright?

It seems strange that men have actually been to the moon and walked about on it. In some ways I wish they hadn't: it turns out to be rather a dull place, after all. Not at all like Mouse's visit to the moon; d'you remember?

Aren't you too big for that story now? All right, then, you lie down and I'll tell it again. If I can remember it. If I leave any bits out, you remind me.

It was an unusually bright moonlight night along the ditch. Mouse had been lying in his little bed for some time, but he was finding it very difficult to go to sleep. The moonlight was streaming into the hole, and just outside he could see a large moth, obviously very wide awake, with its proboscis unrolled into a low-trailing bloom of honeysuckle. The scent came drifting into the hole, a nightingale was singing in the woods about a quarter of a mile away, and the active feeling of the night made Mouse feel more like writing poetry than going to sleep.

'Perhaps I could write an ode?' thought Mouse. 'I'm not quite sure what an ode is, actually. Still, I suppose anyone can try. The moon's bright enough for writing and much too bright for sleeping.'

He got out of bed and rummaged round for a pencil. He found one lying next to yesterday's shopping list, and as there was nothing on the back of the list, he smoothed it out and put it on

the floor beside the bed.

'I wonder how you begin?' he thought, looking up at the moon, and wondering, not for the first time, what all the dark streaks and marks on its face could possibly be. 'Perhaps they're holes, like this one. I suppose there might be mice up there, too, come to that. And cheese. If I were a real poet, I'd know what to say about the moon.

If I were someone great, like Milton,
I'd say the moon was made of – er – Stilton.

How splendid! What a marvellous opening! Arresting, I call that. I shall write it down.'

Mouse sucked his pencil for a few minutes and then added another couplet.

If I wrote poems like John Clare,
I'd say the moon looked cold and bare.

'This is good stuff. Perhaps Professor Carstairs will help me to get it published. I might even get some money for it, you never know.' Thoroughly inspired, Mouse gazed once more at the moon and continued.

If I could write an ode like Keats,
I'd say the moon was made of sweets,
And if I had the fire of Shelley,
I'd say the moon was – er – was made of *jelly*!

Mouse squeaked excitedly and scribbled like mad on the shopping list.

But now it seemed indeed that something extremely odd was happening to the moon; or at any rate to the moonlight, which seemed to have changed its quality, to have become still and, in some strange way, firm – almost as though it really were made of jelly. The surface of the moonbeam itself appeared to be faintly gleaming, nacreous like mother-of-pearl, and Mouse, looking at it, thought that he could even see an indistinct reflection of his own tail. Gingerly putting out one paw, he touched the moonbeam. It felt cool and firm, with a moist, slightly crisp surface; rather like jelly, in fact; or like a water-ice.

'This is very strange,' said Mouse to himself. He went cautiously nearer and sniffed it, but it had no smell. 'I wonder – I wonder whether it would bear me?'

He went round to where the foot of the moonbeam touched the floor and cautiously clambered on it. It wobbled slightly – rather like a bar in the gym – but otherwise seemed perfectly stable. Looking upward, he could see its glistening length stretching out of the hole and away into the dark-blue sky.

'Well, I shall climb up it,' said Mouse. 'Because it's there,' he added after a few moments.

He went out through the mouth of the hole as though up a ramp, fascinated by the completely smooth, bright path stretching ahead. It was certainly easy enough to keep going, for the moonbeam was no colder than the surface of a glass, and featureless and free from obstacles as a frozen pond. It wasn't very wide, certainly, but Mouse was so small himself that there seemed no risk of falling off. The only thing that made him feel distinctly odd was his realization that the moonbeam was transparent, so that he could look down through it and see the woods and fields. They were a very long way below – and getting lower every minute. They made him feel giddy, so he decided to stop looking down and keep his nose pointing upward and straight ahead.

'I'm like Tom Kitten,' muttered Mouse. 'I can't go back. I might fall. All the same, I'd rather be here than up any old chimney. It's a lovely night and very warm.'

The moon was getting nearer now – indeed, filling the whole view ahead – and much larger than he had ever seen it before. There certainly were holes in it and – good gracious! what was that faint, delicious whiff from the sky? No mistaking that – it really was Stilton! The moon *was* made of Stilton!

'Poets are the unacknowledged legislators of mankind,' thought Mouse with satisfaction, put his nose down and began to run.

A few minutes later he stepped resolutely off

the moonbeam and found himself on the surface of the moon. All around him lay the beautiful plains of aromatic cheese, yellow and green, faintly luminous except where they were rifted and pitted with greyish-brown cracks, just as good Stilton should be.

'Then felt I like some watcher of the skies,' cried Mouse, 'when a –'

At this moment he heard a light scuffling behind him and, turning quickly, saw a Moon Mouse, bright blue from nose to backside, with a long, green tail.

Well, it was a bit like Monostatos and Papageno. Each mouse looked at the other in consternation and then bolted – Mouse round a lump of cheese and the Moon Mouse down his hole. After a minute or two, however, Mouse pulled himself together.

'After all,' he thought, 'tom-tits are blue – and rhapsodies; one of them, anyway; and so's the Danube – or that's what I've always heard. So why not a blue mouse? Anyway, he doesn't seem very fierce.'

And forthwith Mouse, humming a tune to keep up his spirits, marched back to the Moon Mouse's hole and called, 'I'm an Earth Mouse – an explorer. Can I come in?'

Once the Moon Mouse realized that he was alone and not fierce, he became most friendly, and showed Mouse round his hole. Mouse had been wondering what it could be like to live with cheese all round you – cheese walls, cheese floor – but then he discovered that in fact the cheese only extended underground about two inches and that underneath the moon was just soil and stones, the same as the Earth.

'And how do you manage for water?' he asked.

The Moon Mouse looked slightly alarmed.

'Water?' he said, 'Oh, good heavens, we never drink water! We don't need it – Moon Mice don't.'

'Isn't there any?' asked Mouse, who was beginning to feel distinctly thirsty.

The Moon Mouse shook his head.

'Only milk,' he said, 'and that's round at the back of the moon. There's a lot of milk there – lakes of it – but round this side it's all turned into cheese. That's why we live on this side. We never go round the back.'

'Why not?' asked Mouse.

The Moon Mouse looked very nervous. 'It's the cats!' he replied in a low voice. 'They're awfully fierce! All the cats live that side – for the milk, you see. I'd advise you to keep away, or you'll never get back to that Earth of yours.'

'But I must have a drink,' said Mouse. 'Where I come from we have cats too, but we generally manage to dodge them.'

'Well, it's different here,' replied the Moon Mouse. 'There's very little cover apart from our holes, you see.'

However, Mouse soon got so much thirstier that he decided to risk it and have a crafty shufti round the back of the moon. So off he went, pattering along, round the lunar curve, until all of a sudden, and quite unexpectedly, he found himself on the shore of the Great Milk Lake – Mare Magnum Lactiferum. There it lay, still as snow and far smoother, yet not so white as snow nor nothing near, because of the beautiful cream covering all the surface. As Mouse, entranced, gazed across it to the further shore, he saw two great creatures, far off, come gliding down among the rocks and crouch, lapping, on their haunches. He had just had a drink himself and was licking his whiskers and thinking what excellent cream it was, when to his horror he saw a third animal, just like the other two, slinking towards him. It had orange fur, sharp, purple teeth and a long, very thin tail which looked as if it were articulated, like a bicycle chain.

'Stop!' shouted this dreadful creature. 'You're trespassing! I want a word with you!'

'The hell you do!' thought Mouse, running like a collier's whippet. 'Oh gosh! I wish I'd never come!'

It was a terrible pursuit, and Mouse was breathless and at his wits' end when, as he came round again to the nearer side of the moon, he suddenly saw the moonbeam – his moonbeam –

shining bravely out of the cheesy ground and into the night sky. Without stopping for an instant, he leapt out on its smooth surface and began sliding downward, nose first.

It was a frightening slither – much worse than any slide in a playground, because there were no raised sides to the moonbeam and Mouse didn't dare to try to slow himself down, because he was afraid the Moon Cat must be following. But then, as he shot downwards, he heard a scrabbling and miaowling up above, and the Moon Cat shouted, 'All *right*, Mouse, all *right*! I'm going back to switch off the moon! And we'll see how you like *that*!'

'Bells and buckets!' thought Mouse. 'Switch off the moon! And I must weigh all of an ounce! I'm afraid there won't be enough air resistance to save me! I wish I hadn't drunk all that cream!'

Far away below, he could see the quiet, moonlit trees and meadows of Earth rushing up towards him at increasing speed. Now he could see his own field, his own ditch and the moonbeam shining into his hole. As he shot over the beeches, he dug in his claws and leaned backwards with all his might, to try to slow down. And then – then the moon was switched off and

he went flying head over heels through the cowparsley.

There was a bump. Mouse found himself sitting on the floor of the hole. The sun, just risen, was shining greenly through the leaves outside and beside him lay his pencil and his glorious ode.

'Did I dream it?' said Mouse. He burped loudly. 'The cream – the cheese – well, I suppose that's what they call internal evidence. I've had a very adventurous night. Whoever would have thought there was so much going on up there in the moon? My tablets – where's that pencil?

If I could write like Philip Larkin,
I'd say the moon was worth remarkin'.

No wonder I feel sleepy. I think I'll have a snooze and a late breakfast.'

And so saying, Mouse climbed back into bed and fell fast asleep. And that was all until next time.

Look, Antares is down. I think even Mr Jackson's gone to bed now, Julie, and I know I'm going there myself. I can hear Mummy's bath running out. I hope you feel a bit sleepier. No hurry in the morning, anyway.

=A Hundred Times=

I say, Jackson, can you help me with this beastly thing? Only old Sopwith says if I don't show it up right tomorrow he's going to keep me in half the afternoon, and then I shan't be able to play in the match against West Downs.

Well, I s'pose it *was* my fault, sort of. I never can do maths. and old Sopwith's had his knife into me all this term, really – me and Reynolds. And this morning he was talking about these rotten cube roots and chalking it all up on the board, you know, and gassing away nineteen to the dozen, and Reynolds and me were playing noughts and crosses under the desk. And suddenly old Sopwith whipped round and said, 'So therefore – h'mm, h'mm – the cube root of 125 is – h'mm, h'mm – what, Burton?' And of course I hadn't a clue. And then he came down and dragged out the beastly bit of paper with all the noughts and crosses on it – he must have known all the time – and of course Reynolds owned up as well; and old Sopwith said, 'Since you – h'mm, h'mm – evidently don't wish to be instructed by me, you can – h'mm, h'mm – instruct yourselves better, no doubt. Tomorrow at first lesson you can both inform me what are the cube roots of 9,261, 29,791 and 68,921.' What? Yes, of course those are the right figures. Here, look – he made us write them down. Well, I can't see anything to *laugh* at, Jackson. And if we don't get them right

he's going to make us do cube roots all tomorrow afternoon, dash it!

Well, no, I didn't *pick* on you, Jackson; but you're the best chap at maths. in the lower school and me and Reynolds just thought – Look, tell you what! I know a super story – really clever – if you'll do the cube roots I'll tell it to you, how's that? You'll hear it first? Oh, all right, then.

Well, a long time ago there was a king, and one day he was out hunting, you see; and he lost his way in the forest. And after a bit he came to a peasant's hut. The peasant was chopping wood just outside the door, so the king got off his horse and went to ask him the way back to the palace. The peasant was quite a cheery sort of bloke, not at all nervous or anything to find himself talking to the king, and the long and short of it was that the king ended up in his hut, having a drink with him. As they were chatting, the king said, 'How much money do you earn a day?' and the peasant answered, 'Four drachmas, your Majesty.' (Or four shillings, Jackson, or four piastres, or anything you like. It doesn't really matter.) 'What do you do with them?' asked the king. 'Well,' said the peasant, 'the first one I eat; the second I invest; the third I give back and the fourth I throw away.'

The king found this very puzzling and he thought it over for a bit. At last he said, 'I don't understand at all. You can't puzzle the king. It's

not allowed. You must explain.'

'Well, it's like this, your Majesty,' said the peasant. 'With the first one I feed myself; with the second I feed my children, who'll have the task of caring for me when I'm old; with the third I feed my father, and so repay him for all he's done for me; and with the fourth I feed my wife, and therefore I say I throw it away, because I get no profit from it.'

The king thought this was very amusing; and he gave the peasant a piece of gold and said, 'Promise me you won't tell anyone else the answer to that riddle until you've seen my face a hundred and one times.' Just at that moment one of the royal counsellors, who'd come out with the king on the hunting party, happened to come riding by the peasant's hut, so the king joined him and rode off home.

The next day at dinner, the king said to the queen and all the counsellors who were dining with him, 'I know a jolly good riddle and I bet none of you can answer it. A peasant earns four drachmas a day. The first he eats; the second he invests; the third he gives back and the fourth he throws away. How do you explain that?'

None of the counsellors could answer the riddle, and the king was so pleased with himself that he said he'd give two hundred gold pieces to anyone who could guess it by that evening. They all went off scratching their heads and the king

felt that just for once he'd succeeded in scoring off them, because quite often he used to feel that they were all a lot cleverer than he was and this annoyed him.

Now of course one of the counsellors at dinner was the one who'd happened to ride past the peasant's hut the day before and come upon the king having a drink with the peasant. And he thought to himself, 'I wonder whether that old peasant mightn't have had something to do with all this?' So he got on his horse and rode off back to the peasant's hut.

When he got there, he told the peasant about the king's riddle and asked him the answer. The peasant said he couldn't tell him the answer, because he'd promised the king he wouldn't. Finally he said he'd only tell the counsellor the answer in return for ninety-nine gold pieces. The old counsellor gave him what he asked, 'cause of course he stood to win two hundred, you see, and off he rode back to the palace.

That evening, when the king and everybody were together again in the palace, the counsellor said, 'Your Majesty, I've found out the answer to your riddle.' And then he said it, just as the peasant had told him.

'Why, that dirty, rotten peasant!' said the king. 'He must have told you! You couldn't have guessed it by yourself!'

'That's true, your Majesty,' answered the

counsellor. 'He *did* tell me, otherwise I shouldn't have got it. But all the same, I think you still owe me two hundred gold pieces.'

Well, the king paid up, but he felt so cross about it that he had his horse brought round that very minute, and off he rode to the peasant's hut. As soon as he got there, he banged like hell on the door and when the peasant came out he said, 'Look, what the devil's going on? You promised me you wouldn't tell anyone else the answer to that riddle until you'd seen my face a hundred and one times, and the next thing I know you've told it to that blithering counsellor! What's the big idea? I've a good mind to have you strung up!'

'Why, your Majesty,' answered the peasant. 'I've kept my promise faithfully. When you did me the honour of coming to my hut yesterday, that was when I saw your face once. Then you very generously gave me a gold piece when you left, and that had your face on it, so that was twice. And then your old counsellor, bless him, he gave me another ninety-nine gold pieces, and I can assure your Majesty that I counted them and looked at each one of them very carefully, as my old wife can testify, for she saw me do it.'

The king was so tickled with the peasant's cunning that he made him head forester and after that, whenever he had a problem that was too much for him, he often used to sneak out of the palace and ask the peasant's advice.

So you see, Jackson, I just thought – What? Oh, *no* Jackson, of *course* I didn't mean *you* were a peasant! Oh, you *might* tell me, honestly! Oh, you *might*! 21, 31 and 41? Honestly? What a blinking swiz! But suppose old Sopwith asks how we did it? How d'you actually *do* cube roots, Jackson?

THE ROBIN

Sermons are too long when you're seven, aren't they? As a matter of fact, they're sometimes too long when you're thirty-seven; and I dare say if Grandpa were here he might say 'when you're sixty-seven'. Don't worry – you've done me a good turn. Anyway, there's no virtue in trying to listen to a lot of stuff you can't be expected to understand. Padre Wood's coming to tea on Tuesday, and he'll tell you the same thing himself, I dare say.

Let's sit down in the sun, shall we, on this nice, flat tombstone, and wait for them to come out? I don't suppose they'll be very long. Whose tombstone is it, I wonder? Let's have a look.

'Beneath this stone are deposited the mortal remains of Thomasina Frances, beloved wife of Horatio James Cremorne, physician, of St Bartholomew's Hospital in London and of this parish, who departed this life in her 70th year, on 23rd April, in the year of Our Lord 1795. A cherished mother, an amiable spouse and a congenial friend, she deserved and obtained the admiration and esteem of the whole society. "There shall be no more death, for the former things are passed away."' Well, I think poor old Dr Cremorne must have taken a lot of trouble over that, don't you? I suppose he wrote it himself. It may sound a bit old-fashioned now, but I'm sure his feelings were just as real as anyone's today.

Look, there's a robin – over on that flowering currant bush. I've got a dog biscuit here in my pocket – I generally carry one on Sundays, for old Tinker – Mrs Fleetwood's Tinker, you know. Well, I know it's Good Friday – same thing, only different, as they say. Let's break a bit up and see if he'll come and take the crumbs. We'll scatter them on this other tombstone, over here. Now back to Mrs Cremorne, and see what happens.

Yes, there you are, he's on it, sharp as a knife! Isn't he tame? There's usually a resident robin in a churchyard, especially one that isn't full. They're quiet, undisturbed places, you see, with flowers and bushes that attract insects, and of course whenever the sexton has any digging to do, the robin can lend him a hand with the worms and beetles. In fact, it may very well be the sexton that's made this fellow so tame.

Robins are lucky, you know. No one in his senses harms a robin. There's an old legend about him. My nurse – Constance Cripps, her name was – told me the story a long time ago. She didn't say she believed it, but when I asked her she wouldn't say she didn't.

She said that long ago, on that first Good Friday, when Jesus was condemned by Pontius Pilate, there was a robin living near the gate of Jerusalem. He used to peck about beside the road and pick up crumbs from the camel-drivers and

market people who were always coming and going. Well, he saw the crowd coming out of the gate that morning, and the soldiers in the middle of it all, and he saw poor Jesus and the other two dragging their crosses up the road. Of course he didn't know what it was all about, but he could see that everyone was being unkind to Jesus and shouting and throwing things, and he felt sorry for him, because he thought he looked a kind sort of man and because he was all alone and helpless among the soldiers.

The robin was frightened of the noise and the crowd, but all the same he couldn't help wondering what was going to happen, so he flew along in the hedges and bushes beside the road and kept up with the soldiers. When they got to Calvary he stayed a little way off, but he was near enough to see what happened. After a time he felt he couldn't bear to stay there and not try to help Jesus, so although he was still frightened he flew up to the cross and began trying to pull out the nails. Of course he couldn't do it – they only hurt his beak – but after trying as hard as he could, he flew up to Jesus's head and began pulling out the thorns.

One of the soldiers picked up a stone to throw at the robin, but the centurion told him to stop it, and said that no one was to hurt the robin or drive him away. We know that this centurion felt sorry for Jesus and that during that day he became convinced that he was the son of God, because three of the four gospels all say so. The gospels don't tell his name – any more than they give the names of the wise men – but in all the old legends and stories his name is Longinus.

Before he died, Jesus blessed the robin and promised that for ever after, whenever they saw him, people would remember what he had done. He was all covered with Jesus's blood, which had dried on his breast feathers, and from that day to this his breast has remained the colour of dried blood. He was still there at the end of that terrible afternoon, when Longinus and the soldiers took Jesus's body down and gave it to Joseph of Arimathea to lay in the sepulchre. And

as Longinus had fed him and treated him kindly, the robin followed him back to the city and took to living in his garden, where he soon got so tame that he often used to come in through the window to pick up crumbs and bits of food.

Now the legend says – it's part of the King Arthur story, actually, and one day I'll read it to you in Malory – that Longinus and Joseph of Arimathea became great friends and were among the first Christians and followers of the disciples. But after a time they grew afraid of what Pontius Pilate and King Herod might do to them, so they decided to leave the country. In the Middle Ages people used to believe that they sailed together to England, and that with them they brought three things: a piece of the cross, the spear with which Longinus had pierced Jesus's side after he died, and the Holy Grail – the cup which Jesus had blessed at the Last Supper. The legend says that the piece of the cross was planted at Glastonbury in Somerset, and from it sprung up the holy Glastonbury thorn, which was believed to bloom at midnight on Christmas Eve. The Grail was mysteriously received into heaven, but was later revealed to three of King Arthur's knights – Sir Galahad, Sir Bors and Sir Percival – and what became of the spear I don't remember to have heard.

But the robin came to England too. Longinus had become so fond of him and his red breast that he made him a little cage and he sailed with them on the ship, and when they reached England they let him go. And ever since then he's lived near people's houses and brought them good luck, and often he's so tame that he'll come in through the kitchen window and sometimes even feed out of your hand, just like Longinus's robin. If you're digging in the garden he'll come and peck about in the newly-dug ground; and he never leaves England, even in the hardest winter weather. The unluckiest thing you can do is to harm a robin, or let your cat hurt one. When the early settlers went to America, they missed the robin very much – there aren't any over there, you see – so they gave the name 'robin' to another, bigger bird which happens to have a chestnut-coloured breast, although it's not much like the English robin. It's actually a sort of thrush – *turdus migratorius* – and its habits are quite different from our robin's.

Of course we oughtn't to get these legends mixed up with the really important stories in the gospels about Jesus and the disciples. But all the same, they are beautiful and worth remembering, because they show that ordinary, simple people in the old days used to feel very deeply about Jesus and connect things in their own lives and surroundings with him.

Ah, here they all come, look – like sparks up the back of the chimney, as my father used to say. My goodness, look at Mrs Fleetwood's new hat! D'you mind if we just wait a minute or two? I want to have a word with Padre Wood about the new nets for the cricket field.

Prince Meerzat Istvan and the Horse of Dust and Thunder

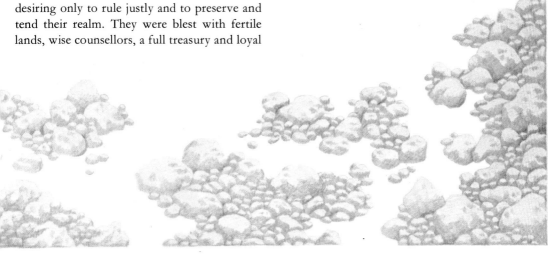

A rt thou asleep, my dear one? Canst thou hear the stream and see the flowers among the green grass?

Dost thou ask who am I? Thou knowest who I am. Lay thy head in my lap, here among the forget-me-nots, for I am come to tell thee a tale in thy sleep. It is but the one tale I tell, and all who sleep hear it.

> Dream, my loved one, stretched at ease
> Under April's hawthorn trees.
> Green the leaves and clear the sky.
> Thou shalt waken by and by.

Once there lived a king and queen, gracious and honourable, loved by their subjects and desiring only to rule justly and to preserve and tend their realm. They were blest with fertile lands, wise counsellors, a full treasury and loyal and valiant warriors: yet they had no child. Many learned men and doctors they consulted to no avail, until at length they heard of a certain sage living in the wilderness, six days' journey beyond the furthest boundary of their kingdom. The king sent messengers with gifts summoning the wise man to court and promising him great rewards: but he returned the presents, and with them his reply that those who sought his help must needs come to him.

So the king and queen made that journey, to the end of their kingdom and beyond, until at last they came in sight of the wise man's dwelling. Then they left their horses with their attendants and walked on, bareheaded and alone, for thus, they had been advised, must all approach him who sincerely desired his help.

When the wise man saw them coming he went out to meet them and, welcoming them gravely and courteously, sat down beside them, in the shade of a flowering tamarisk, to hear their trouble. The king told him of their disappointment and great desire, and of their need for a son to inherit the realm. Having heard all, he said, 'O king, I tell thee that thy wish fulfilled will bring thee grief at last.'

The king, already wearied by the long journey and now troubled to see tears start to the eyes of his beloved queen, felt some impatience and even anger. Yet being a courteous and generous-hearted gentleman, he replied only, 'Honoured sir, thou must allow us to judge for ourself the need of our queen and our subjects. We came not hither to be persuaded against our heart's desire, but to seek thy help in its fulfilment.'

At this the stern old hermit felt pity for the beautiful queen, and promised to enable them to achieve their wish. 'Yet,' said he, 'what God gives, no man can keep; and so wilt thou learn, O king – yea, even thou. Yet because thou hast sought me out in patience and humility, thou hast both constrained and enabled me to help thee. Thy wish will be granted – not by me, but by God. Nay, sir, I need no reward. Go in peace.'

> Dost thou sleep, my love, at ease;
> Hear the murmur of the bees
> And the rustling of the rye?
> Thou shalt waken by and by.

The queen bore a son and the whole kingdom rejoiced, with feasting and bonfires. Prince Meerzat Istvan he was named; and as he grew, strong and healthy, into his second and then his third and fourth year, the king, when his day's work was done (for he worked as hard as any man and harder than many), would often take him in his arms and walk with him upon the great terrace above the palace gardens, singing to him or telling him old tales, and thinking of all that still needed to be done to safeguard the happy and prosperous realm which would one day pass to his splendid young heir. One evening, as he brought him back to the queen, the little boy was fretful and would not stop crying.

'Peace, my dear son,' said the king, 'thou of all lads hast no cause to cry! Behold, I will give thee a great kingdom and all its riches!'

But still the child cried.

'Peace, my young lord,' said the king, tossing him up and down and laughing, 'thou shalt have the most beautiful princess in the world for thy wife, and live with her in a golden palace!'

Yet still the child cried.

'Peace, great prince!' said his father. 'Do but smile, and fall asleep, and I will give thee youth without age and life without death!'

Then the boy ceased crying and fell asleep in his mother's arms.

Before Prince Meerzat Istvan had reached the age of ten, it was already clear that he was full of the promise of great things, for he was both strong and clever, as quick to learn the skills of hunters, horsemen and soldiers as the wisdom of scholars and wise men. The people were glad to feel that the succession was so well assured. He made no enemies; and soon, as a youth, was already able to take part of the burden of the realm from the king's shoulders. The king had determined that on his nineteenth birthday he would appoint him viceroy over three provinces, with his own council to advise and help him. 'For so,' said he, 'he will gain experience and come to understand the responsibilities of a ruler.'

On the day before this birthday, the prince came to his father and said, 'Father, the time has now come for me to ask of thee that gift which thou didst promise; youth without age and life without death.'

'My dear son,' replied the king, 'how strange that thou shouldst recall that evening! It must be more than fifteen years ago! Thou wert scarcely more than a baby, and 'tis true I made thee an idle promise to still thy tears.'

'Yet now must I claim that gift,' said he.

'Nay, thou art jesting!' answered his father. 'How can I or any man give thee what has never been granted to any?'

'Then,' said the prince, 'I must needs set forth and win it for myself. And when I have done so, dear father, I will return and inherit the kingdom, as thou dost desire.'

Forthwith Prince Meerzat Istvan made his way to the royal stables, to choose himself a horse for his journey. Yet as he laid his hand on each in turn, it sank trembling to the ground and he could do nothing with it. When he had gone through the whole stable from one end to the other, he saw a door at the back of the yard where the manure was piled.

'What is beyond that door?' he asked the grooms.

'Why, your royal Highness,' replied one, 'that is nothing but an old shed where the sick and worn-out horses are kept until the knacker comes to collect them. You have already seen all that the royal stables can offer.'

Nevertheless the prince commanded the grooms to open the shed, and there he found a thin, broken-down horse, covered with sores and too weak to stand. He was turning away when the horse raised its head and whispered, 'I am Levom Leseur Melikaern, the steed of dust and thunder!'

As the prince stood still in amazement, he realized that none of those about him had perceived or understood that the horse had spoken. Caring nothing for their stares and covert laughter, he fell on his knees beside the horse and asked, 'What must I do?'

'Go to thy father,' replied the horse, 'and ask of him the arms that he himself bore as a youth. Then thou must tend and groom me seven days with thine own hands, and feed me well, for it is I and I alone that can bear thee where thou art resolved to go.'

Sleep tranquil, my dearest, my love. Dost thou feel the soft breeze on thy cheek? Dost thou know the sun is high? Thou shalt waken by and by.

Then, at his son's request, the king caused to be opened all the cupboards and cellars of the royal armoury, and the prince searched them by candlelight, among cobwebs and shadows. At last he found the arms and armour which his father had borne as a youth, rusty and long-disused, with many of the straps and clasps worn out. With his own hands he repaired, oiled and cleaned all, until the joints moved smoothly and the armour shone in the sun. And for seven days, with help from none, he tended the horse and slept beside it in the straw of the shed. But indeed during this time he slept little; and what the horse said to him no one knows.

On the eighth day he led the horse to the royal forge, shod it himself and, having buckled on his arms, led it out to the great terrace above the gardens. Here he bade farewell to the weeping king and queen and to the court and the royal counsellors, who shook their heads and felt such disappointment that they could scarcely find a blessing to bestow upon him. Then he rode away, and with him went fifty warriors and a train of servants, whom the king had commanded to follow him and guard him with their lives.

When he was come to the wilderness on the borders of the kingdom – that same wilderness where, years before, his mother and father had sought out the wise man – he dismissed all his followers, telling them to take back his blessing to his mother, and journeyed on alone, letting the horse carry him whither it would. After twelve days and nights he came, beyond the wilderness, to a wide, barren plain which was all covered with the bones of dead men.

'Now,' said he to the horse, 'seeing that there's none here but thee and me, thou must tell me why we're come hither and what it is we have to do.'

'Master,' replied the horse, 'we are now in the domain of the witch Gheonoea, than whom is no more evil being in the world. Once she was a beautiful girl, until the curse of her parents, whom she hated and betrayed, fell like bitter ice upon her and turned her to a living pestilence. She is even now hastening hither to destroy thee, but have no fear. Only make ready and trust in thyself and me.'

Then they encamped in that evil place to wait, and one watched while the other slept.

On the second morning Prince Meerzat, wakened by his horse, at once heard an approaching commotion like that of a tempest. Springing up, he saw, far off across the plain, the tree-tops bending as though in a high wind.

'Gheonoea is close, master,' said Levom Leseur Melikaern. 'String thy bow, and have an arrow ready on the string.'

As the terrible witch came trampling through the skulls and bones, scattering them like the dust of summer, Prince Meerzat shot her in the foot and brought her to the ground: and there-

upon she begged mercy of him and promised to do him no harm.

'Do not trust her, master,' said the horse. 'Make her write thee a promise in her own blood!' And this he did.

'Ah, Prince Meerzat,' cried the witch, 'take good care of thy horse, for he is a greater magician than I! But for him I would have slain thee! Now I will feast both thee and him, and give thee shelter besides, for as long as thou dost wish. Thou needs fear no treachery from me.'

Then Gheonoea entertained Prince Meerzat honourably, and he himself healed for her the wound he had inflicted with his arrow. Two days he stayed with her, and she begged him to take for his consort whichever of her three beautiful daughters he might choose; yet he would not, but asked only for advice on the search that he had undertaken. When she saw that she could not keep him and that his horse and he would be

gone come what might, she went with him across the plain to the foot of a range of great mountains; and here she parted from him, only warning him that the way ahead was full of danger.

Dost thou sleep calmly, my love, my cherished one? The cattle stand knee-deep in the noonday stream and the stubble fields are dry. Thou shalt waken by and by.

Long and hard was the passage of the mountains, but his good horse bore the prince ever onward, and at last they came down into another plain, across which ran a paved road. On one side of this the grass grew green, full of flowers and scented herbs, but on the other all was blackened cinders and a waste of ashes, so that Prince Meerzat, as he looked at it, felt a foreboding come upon him in the lonely silence.

'What place is this?' he asked the horse.

'This is the realm of Scorpia, master,' answered the horse, 'sister of Gheonoea. The two sisters cannot live together, so evil are they, and the mountains we have crossed were raised to keep them apart, lest their mutual hatred should destroy the world. Scorpia – ah, the curse of night and hell is upon her, so that she vomits fire and flame! This is why the grass of this plain is burned and withered as far as the eye can see. She has three heads and for this reason none can surprise her, since she never sleeps.'

Then they travelled on across the plain, keeping good watch about them all the while, the prince holding his bow in readiness and often turning to look behind as well as before. But they encountered nothing all that day, nor yet the next.

At length, at dawn on the third day, just as light was coming into the sky, they saw a column of dark smoke, lit ever and anon from within by flashes of fire, which seemed to be rushing towards them across the blackened ground. The prince needed no telling that this must be the onset of the witch Scorpia. Both he and his good horse trembled at the sight, yet despite their fear they stood fast and then, as the witch drew yet nearer, went forward to meet her attack. At the last moment the horse swerved like lightning from the path of the scorching fire and the prince, even as he felt the blistering heat against his side, shot an arrow which transfixed one of the witch's three fearsome heads. With a shriek she fell on the plain, and the smoke and flame about her sank lower and began to lose part of its terrible force. Levom Leseur Melikaern checked his stride and turned back towards her, in order that the prince might shoot again. But before he could do so the witch begged for mercy; and as before, he demanded of her a promise, written in her own blood, that she would do him no harm.

Then she feasted and entertained him as royally as had her sister, and begged him to remain with her and share her realm. But again he refused and, as soon as her wound was healed, parted from her and rode away, glad to leave behind that evil place of destruction. And so, after many miles, the prince and the faithful steed came to a land of eternal spring, where the air was full of the fragrance of great, glowing flowers that bloomed all the year round in meadows fringed by the sea.

Dream on, my dearest heart, my loved one. The sunlight dapples the leaves in the windless afternoon. Lullaby, and lullaby: thou shalt waken by and by.

'Good master, brave master,' then said the horse, 'hitherto we have prospered, but now there lies before us the greatest danger of all: yet with God's help we may overcome it; and so shalt thou win at last thy heart's desire. Not far away stands the palace of Youth without Age and Life without Death, surrounded by a trackless forest, the haunt of monsters and serpents, basilisks and hydras without number. We cannot hope to fight them, nor could we ever pass through those dreadful thickets. If thou art still determined on the adventure, I will not desert thee. We can only try to o'erleap the forest and so come to the palace. Yet much as we have achieved already, I cannot promise that we shall succeed in so desperate a venture as this will be.'

'Nevertheless, let us attempt it,' said the prince, 'for I have always trusted thee and do not believe that thou wilt fail me now.'

So then they rested more than two days, to recover their full strength and to commend themselves to God. And at noon of the third day Levom Leseur Melikaern said to the prince, 'Now must I try the leap, or not at all, for I would become no stronger were I to rest a month. Draw my saddle-girths as tight as thou canst and when thou hast mounted, press thy feet on my neck and not on my flanks, to hinder me as little as possible.'

The prince mounted and the good horse made towards the terrible wood, first at a walk, then at a trot, then a canter and at last at full gallop, the green sods flying like snow from beneath his well-shod hooves. Like a whirlwind of dust and thunder he came to the trees and rose into the air above them. There, beyond and below them, lay the golden palace, shining up from the centre of the wood like a water-lily in a dark pool. High over the forest they flew, the steed's mane streaming in the wind. Yet all his strength was barely enough, for as they came down towards the palace gate, one hind-leg brushed a pendent bough. Instantly the whole forest was filled with clamour and from far and near the monsters came crawling and hissing towards them, so that the prince, for all his resolution, trembled where he sat and almost fell to the ground from fear.

Just as it seemed that all must be lost, there came pacing through the palace gate a tall and stately maiden, bearing in one hand a long staff of ivory. As she raised it aloft, the monsters crept back to their forest lairs, and in the silence the

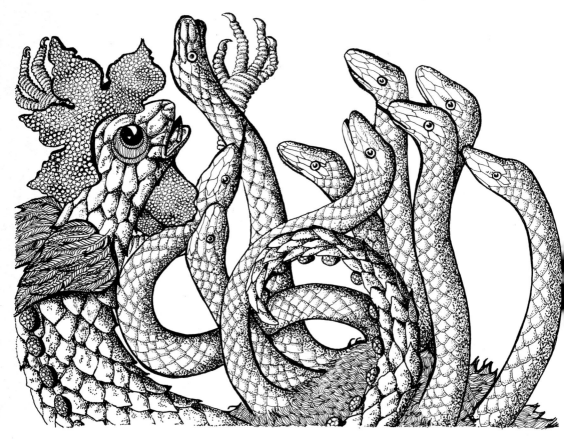

prince dismounted and followed her through the gate, leading his good horse by the bridle. They came into a courtyard, and thence into a great hall of carved stone and cedar-wood, in the centre of which stood a long table, all of ebony, laid with gold plate and candlesticks of silver. Musicians, in silk and pearl, sat playing in the gallery, and six beautiful girls helped Prince Meerzat Istvan to unarm, brought him water and towels and escorted him to a high, carved chair at the head of the table. Levom Leseur Melikaern they led to the stables, where an old, skilful servant groomed, fed and rested him as he deserved.

Then the prince and the maiden feasted together, side by side, and all her household feasted also, and pledged them in white wine and red. When the feasting was done, she led him to an upper room facing westward over the forest. It was filled with the light of sunset; and here they sat together while he told her of his quest and all his hard adventures.

'And what wilt thou have now?' asked she, when at length the tale was done. 'What seekest thou here?'

'I am seeking youth without age and life without death,' replied he.

'Then needst thou journey no further,' she answered, 'for this is the palace of youth without age, and I have awaited thee these eighteen years. I am the princess of life without death, and thine own love.'

So they were married, and Prince Meerzat Istvan dwelt in the golden palace and hunted in the great forest, for his bride bestowed upon him her power over all its dangers.

Yet sleep on, dear heart, and learn the end. Already the sun is lower and the air is cool. Lie still. Indeed, thou canst not choose, yet never ask me why. Thou shalt waken by and by.

How long Prince Meerzat lived in the golden palace cannot be told, for there was no time there, a day was as a year and spring bloomed perpetually. Yet at last there came an evening when he became filled with an overwhelming longing to return home, to see once more his dear mother and father and to walk on the great terrace above the gardens of their palace.

'I did my father wrong,' said he to the princess, 'for I deserted the kingdom which he had planned to safeguard against his death, and the good peasants and citizens who believed that I would come to rule over them as wisely as my father. Return with me to that country, my dearest, for when they see you they will love you as I do, and my father will die happy after all.'

Then she led him again into the upper room overlooking the forest and the sunset and, gazing into his eyes, said, 'Alas, my love, speak no more of this longing. Thousands of years have passed since thy father and mother died. No power in the world can restore time that is fled, leaves that are fallen and snows that are melted. Didst thou not ride to the end of the world to achieve thy dearest wish, and did I not bestow it upon thee with all my heart? If once thou dost leave the palace of youth without age thou wilt never return. See, my love, the sun is setting. Let us feast together in the hall, and then meet in love and sleep as often before.'

Yet he would not heed her, but called the old groom and bade him saddle Levom Leseur Melikaern and prepare all things for his journey. 'For,' said he, 'I repent that I left my dear father despite all that he wished for me and for his kingdom. I will be gone tonight, that I may the sooner return to my love, and to the palace of youth without age.'

'Good master,' said Levom Leseur Melikaern, 'let me, thy dear horse, that never yet misled thee, prevail upon thee to heed the words of the princess. If once thou dost leave the palace, thou wilt never return. Only stay tonight, and in the morning we will speak further of this desire in thy heart.'

'Nay,' said he, 'we must be gone before dark. Thou hast ever been my friend. Wilt thou not bear me, as so often before, over plain and mountain, until we come to my father's kingdom?'

'I will not fail thee, master,' replied the horse. 'But mark well! If thou dost dismount, be it only for a moment, then must I return without thee and we shall never meet again.'

'Trust me,' replied the prince. 'I will not dismount.'

Then he moved his hand to the princess, but she did not see him ride away through the enchanted wood, for her eyes were blinded with tears. Twilight fell and night, yet the horse went on, swift as the wind, and never stumbled.

They came to the plain where had been the scorched and blackened realm of Scorpia, but it was golden with acres of corn stretching away to the gates of a noble city. Prince Meerzat, having ridden into that city, asked one and another concerning Scorpia, but they answered him that Scorpia was a legend of long ago, and that even the oldest could not say whether she had ever truly lived or no. Then he told them that he himself had fought and subdued her, and they laughed, not from discourtesy but thinking that he must needs be speaking in jest. When he rode away he did not notice that his beard and hair had grown white.

They came to the domain of Gheonoea, but where the bones had covered the ground, shepherds were grazing their flocks and men had cut a canal to water the land. He could not understand how the whole region could have changed in a few weeks; nor could they tell him anything of Gheonoea, save that they had never heard of her; and from there he rode away with failing eyesight and hands that trembled on the reins.

They passed through the old hermit's wilderness and so came at last to the land where the prince had been born, but he could not find the palace, nor discover any street or face that he

remembered. At last, by chance, they passed by a graveyard and, looking over the hedge, he saw an overgrown, neglected tomb on which could just be read the almost-obliterated inscription, 'Here lies the king who was father of Prince Meerzat Istvan. At his own command, nought else is here inscribed of his life and deeds.'

When the prince saw that, he dismounted from his horse and flung himself weeping upon the stone. After a time he became aware that the horse was nuzzling his shoulder, and he looked up.

'Master,' said the horse, 'all things come to an end, both good and bad. The time is come at last when thou and I must part. Accept my thanks and blessing for all the good times we saw together.'

The prince flung his arms about his faithful horse, unsaddled him and took off his bit and bridle. Then the horse went away swiftly, for he could not bear to look back at the decrepit old man lying on the mossy stone.

A cold rain began to fall, and Prince Meerzat Istvan looked about for shelter. Not far off stood an old, ruined mosque and, making his way to it, he turned the ring of the door and pushed it open on its rusty hinges. As he entered a voice said, 'Welcome, Prince! Hadst thou kept me waiting longer, I also would have perished.'

Then his death, who was himself shrivelled like a withered leaf, laid hands on Prince Meerzat and he became bones and dust, while high on a silver birch a thrush sang in the rain.

Thou hast slept well, my dearest. The tale is done, and now it is time to waken for ever. There is but one tale, and thou hast dreamed it as I bid thee. Mount thy good horse and be gone; yet bless me, if thou wilt, before I sleep.